Praise for *Conversations in Singapore*

'An invaluable book which reminds us that we define ourselves by our choices. Choose to read this.'
—*Dr John Scally, PhD, Assistant Professor,*
Trinity College Dublin, Ireland

'It is difficult to answer the question: "What is true success?" But Michael's conversations have shown me what true success means to me, and you have to read them too to learn what true success means for *you*.'
—*Dr Imre Gombköto, PhD, Associate Professor,*
University of Miskolc, Hungary

'In the classic book *One Thousand and One Nights,* Scheherazade married a king who had killed a thousand wives after just one night together. Queen Scheherazade, to stay alive, tells a new story each night to the king. In this new classic, Michael Daly invites the reader to consider how to live a life worth living. In his book *Conversations in Singapore: Searching for True Success on the Silk Road, One Question at a Time,* Michael presents his muse, the strange and remarkable Parandin.

Parandin, unlike Scheherazade, does not tell stories, but asks penetrating questions of Michael that encourage him to seek answers within himself. Michael weaves his meetings with Parandin in with another story: his journey on the Silk Road. Offering suggestions, insights and courage, Michael's book will inspire readers to find their own truth about who they are, where they are going and how to be successful in their journey. And

like Scheherazade, this book will leave the reader to discover a thousand and one tales of who they can be.'
—*Professor Jerry Gale, PhD, Department of Human Development and Family Science, Director of the Family Therapy Doctoral Program, University of Georgia, USA*

'In this his second book, Michael has once again managed to surprise me. Here he gives us the possibility to have an insight on the heritage of Hotel Falah, giving us the blessing of motivation. Following the story of his personal growth and success while staying there, we have the benefit of being guided through our own personal achievements. This is the best book on life-recipes: it defines the right ingredients, determines the best processes and yet gives total freedom of individual choice in how to live a life of true success. I am really looking forward to reading his third book!'
—*Professor Domagoja Buljan Barbača, PhD, Head of Department of Finance and Accounting, University of Split, Croatia*

'A great story from the Silk Road: once you open the book, you cannot stop reading until you get the whole story, the whole message and the whole wisdom. Every reader will benefit from having read *Conversations in Singapore*. It is a story which had to be shared, a book which had to be written, and a message which has to be read. . . . Michael is a great storyteller and in this book he definitely has a story to tell. It is like reading Paulo Coelho, but this time it's non-fiction.'
—*Dr Ing. Michal Menšík, PhD, Vice-Rector for External Relations, Moravian University College, Olomouc, Czech Republic*

'Michael Daly is one of the right people to move us forward to find out what true success is, and his book is the perfect way to show clearly how we can reach true success by ourselves.'
—*Dr Ferkan Kaplanseren, PhD, Associate Professor, İzmir Dokuz Eylul University, Turkey*

PRAISE FOR *THE SIX TRAITS OF SELF-LEADERSHIP: HOW TO CREATE A LIFE OF SUCCESS AND HAPPINESS*

'Some public-spirited individual ought to send this book to Leo Varadkar.'

—*Gene Kerrigan, journalist and author*

'One of the smartest books you will ever get to read.'

—*Professor Jim Blythe, Cardiff*

'If you read one book this year, make it this one – it has it all. It will show how you can bring success and happiness to your life and work so as to truly live the life you want to have.'

—*Nick Williams, internationally acclaimed author and inspired entrepreneur, London*

'I recently experienced two moments of enlightenment – listening to Michael's lectures and reading his book on self-leadership. A simplicity of recommendations leading to peace between your mind and heart, a clear vision of your own life and encouragement to immediately turn your thoughts to the inner belief that 'everything is going to work out just right!' You cannot remain at the same stage of your life journey as you were before opening the first pages of this book.'

—*Jolanta Preidiene, Head of International Department, Vilnius University of Applied Sciences, Lithuania*

'*The Six Traits of Self-Leadership* is an excellent book, which I highly recommend to anyone who wants to achieve their personal and professional goals. It provides a simple approach to success and happiness, something most of us want. It reveals the Six Traits that will make you more effective. This book is easy to follow and very inspiring. One of the most powerful and insightful books I've ever read!'

—Professor Ana Paula Lopes,
University of Oporto, Portugal

'Michael Daly has given us an outstanding prescription for getting the kind of satisfaction we want from our lives. In his *The Six Traits of Self-Leadership: How to Create a Life of Success and Happiness*, he has shown how satisfaction is not just about some outsider telling us what to do but really about self-leadership, the way to real personal happiness. Michael gives us the keys to self-leadership with his six traits and illustrates each with down-to-earth examples. The ideas are easily accessible and presented in a friendly style that anyone can understand.'

—Professor Alan Zimmerman,
City University of New York

'This book is both moving and practical. It also reflects the personal experience of the author – a self-leader I admire and respect. It is a fantastic read and gives exceptional everyday-life examples for the reader to put straight into practice. This is a book that will make an impact and it is a must read. So, let it act as your personal assistant and manual as you *create a life of success and happiness* for *The Six Traits of Self-Leadership* shows you how.'

—Professor María José Del Pino Espejo,
University Pablo de Olavide, Seville, Spain

'Have you ever asked the question: what do I need to be successful? The answer is healthy self-confidence, calmness and awareness. You achieve self-confidence through *Bildung*. *Bildung* is translated literally as 'higher education'. *Bildung* is what's left over when you subtract your lessons learned from your knowledge.

Bildung is active! *Bildung* is not a customer relationship. It is not "edutainment" or a passive education where you learn a lot. It's all up to you!

Calmness means: Don't go charging in. Lay back, think for a while before you act. One night is all it takes. Be aware. Look into the eyes of your partners. Do they understand your message? In order to understand more, read this book!

—*Professor Dr Ing. Gerd Mühlenbeck,*
Heidelberg, Germany

'*The Six Traits of Self-Leadership* makes for great reading. It will inspire readers to reach their full potential in life, regardless of age, education or profession. The style is easy and personal. Not only does the author make a valuable synthesis of ideas from different fields – psychology, time management and entrepreneurship – but he also gives readers advice from his own experience or that of his clients. The book is practical, filled with inspiring thoughts and quotes, written with determination, passion and a sense of humour.'

—*Dr Anda Gheorghiu, Associate Professor,*
Hyperion University Bucharest and Internal Auditor,
Romanian National Ombudsman

Conversations in Singapore

First published in 2019 by
Liberties Press
1 Terenure Place | Terenure | Dublin 6W | Ireland
Tel: +353 (0) 86 853 8793
www.libertiespress.com

Distributed in the United States and Canada by
Casemate IPM | 1950 Lawrence Road | Havertown | Pennsylvania
19083 | USA
T: (610) 853 9131 | E: casemate@casematepublishers.com

Copyright © Michael E. Daly
The author asserts his moral rights.
ISBN (print): 978-1-912589-04-3
ISBN (e-book): 978-1-912589-05-0

2 4 6 8 10 9 7 5 3 1
A CIP record for this title is available from the British Library.
Cover design by Roudy Design
Printed in Dublin by Sprint Print

Conversations in Singapore

Searching for True Success on the Silk Road,
One Question at a Time

Michael E. Daly

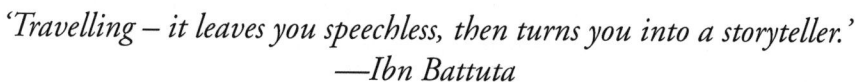

'Travelling – it leaves you speechless, then turns you into a storyteller.'
—Ibn Battuta

For Michelle, Ashley, Brendan, Conor, Leah and Emma Daly

Contents

ACKNOWLEDGEMENTS

There are so many people to thank who either made this journey to the finished book possible or have helped in bringing this book from manuscript to print. In no particular order, and fully aware that I will have missed many, they are as follows.

Thanks to Daniela, David and the rest of you who made the journey from London to Sydney possible. You know who you are; thank you.

Thanks to Anne McFadden, for giving me the time and space to work on this book at her place having got to Sydney, and Dermot O'Rourke, for giving me the time and space to finish this book at his place in the midlands, after I returned to Ireland.

Heartfelt thanks to my sister, sisters-in-law, brothers and brother-in-law, Mary, Maureen, Charlotte, John, Joseph, Brendan and Karl.

Heartfelt thanks to Gerry McLarnon, Allyson Lambert, Brendan Garland, Lilly Daly, Pauline Malone, Declan Hogan, James Russell, Patrick Russell and Brendan Daly for all their support.

Thanks to Mark, Sinead, Saoirse and Caoimhe Foley, Craig and Wendy, Jenny, Alan and all their gang, great neighbours; I am so grateful to have them.

Thanks to my mother Mary, who never questioned my sanity (not to me, anyway!) when I told her I was travelling to so many unknown countries. In my loneliest moments, I always knew I had somewhere loving and caring to go back to whenever I wanted; this is not something everyone has, yet is something for which I shall be eternally grateful. To my father, John, your good and honest life and your (untimely, yet) graceful death inspired the hidden dimensions of my life and revealed what it is to be truly successful.

Big thanks to the very, very talented editor that is Leda Sammarco, who turned this into the book that it is. Thanks too to the copy editor, Jane Collinson, whose great work so enhanced the writing of this book. Heartfelt thanks to Seán O'Keeffe and all the team at Liberties Press for doing such a great job in turning out this, the finished book.

Writing this book has been both wonderful and bittersweet. I have lived in Hotel Falah every day since leaving it – at least in my mind. I will miss the hotel and, in particular, Parandin, dearly, as I now move on with enthusiasm and excitement as this book is published and the story within is put out there into the world.

I am all too aware that I have clambered on the shoulders of giants in the writing of this book, and I can only say that I do so with the utmost respect and reverence, and I truly hope that I have done their ideas, truths and sacred beliefs justice in such a short space.

Preface

In 2014 I published my first book, *Six Traits of Self-leadership: How to Create a Life of Success and Happiness*, to encourage and guide people in reaching their full potential and achieving their dreams. Essentially it was a handbook for those who *know* what they want to do with their life and the success they want, but who are just not sure how to achieve it. (The title was changed to 'The Six Traits of Self-leadership' and was re-published in May 2018; a summary of the six traits appears at the end of this book.) The six traits of self-leadership are intended to guide people in making the success they want for their life a reality.

I felt blessed to receive such positive feedback on the book, but then some people started to say to me: 'Michael, I want to be successful, but I don't know what true success even means to me.' So, I considered the question: what is true success? The more I thought about it, the more I felt I needed to answer this question in my second book. The gods conspired in my favour when it became possible for me to take six months out from work and everyday living to reflect on and answer this question. These six months out were a privilege, and it was my goal to make full use of them to write a follow-up book on what it was to know true success in all areas of one's life.

The intention was to write this book while travelling in a specially designed truck with fourteen other passengers on a twenty-two-week overland journey from London to Sydney, taking in the Silk Road from Istanbul in Turkey to the end of the Great Wall in China. The Silk Road has been a network of routes and a way of traveling between China and the capital of the Roman Empire since the second-century bc. Nowadays it is known as 'The Silk Road: The Way of Dialogue, Mutual Understanding, and Rapprochement of Cultures'. It gained this name because of the lucrative Asian silk that was both transported and traded along its route, which in time was to turn into an extensive transcontinental network. The Silk Road also became a route for the cultural trade of philosophies, sciencific knowledge, technologies and religions among the civilisations it passed through. It has played a major role in the development and opening up of many long-distance political and economic relations between cultures.

This journey was to involve travelling through some of the world's most inhospitable regions and most difficult terrains, including the Tajikistan-Afghanistan border. It was a daunting route to many places I had never heard of before. Camping would often be the only means of accommodation available in such desolate environments.

But as I spent more and more time on the road, the book was just not happening for me. A lot of writing was being done, but it did not seem to be getting to the heart of what I needed to write. Panic set in. Yes, I was seeing amazing sights, meeting so many great people, staying in places I may never get to stay in again, and writing in unbelievable and stunningly beautiful spots. Yet the book was not coming together. My agent wanted more of a historical and academic point of view of what was seen as true success down through the ages. Was it time to leave and focus on the writing completely – and give the publisher what they wanted? Yes, it was heartbreaking to even contemplate leaving; maybe I had to leave, to give the time required solely to writing. After a sleepless night, the decision was made. I was going to leave and focus on the writing – yet it was not to be what the agent wanted, as this just did not sit right with me. Yes to a book on success, only not from an academic viewpoint. The two people whom I had become closest to on the journey were to be told first, out of respect for our growing friendship, after all our adventures together on the truck as we travelled the Silk Road.

Having told my friends, they were both sad that our friendship and support for each other as we travelled together would come to a premature end. They were disappointed for me on a personal level, too, that the writing was not happening, but they fully understood that I could only give the time to writing by leaving, and not finishing the journey on the Silk Road and then going on to Sydney.

Having dealt with the emotions of my leaving, it was time to get practical: inform the group leader, organise transport to the airport and get a flight to somewhere where I could devote the necessary time to writing. But then something unexpected happened. One of my new friends, who had made their career in the hotel industry, arranged for me to stay in a hotel in Singapore where they were owed a favour: they were passing this favour on to me. My friend told me it was a beautiful hotel (I was only to realise how beautiful when I got there), and the booking could not be made straight away. The first and only date they could give me was the very date we as a group had planned to be in Singapore on our way to Sydney anyway. So I could continue writing (even if it was not what the agent wanted), complete the Silk Road with the group, and then go to Singapore and finish the book there. It was a luxury hotel, she explained, but I would not be charged the normal price for staying there. I would get all the time I needed to write.

The only thing was, my life, and the book I had set out to write, were to change utterly, and amazingly, while I was staying at Hotel Falah in Singapore. It is true to say that during these travels I met some of the kindest, most hospitable and interesting people one could ever encounter. One in particular, Parandin, whom I was to meet at Hotel Falah, allowed me to enter into her world.

This was a world in which she shared with me the knowledge, wisdom and profound insight (developed over many generations and handed down to her) into the true meaning of what it is to be successful in life. She came from a tradition of people who were passionate about supporting and encouraging people to live lives of true success. They believed that, from ancient theology to contemporary psychology, our words shape our story and this becomes the framework for our behaviours; and our behaviours determine the way we lead our life, and the success we have. That the story we tell *about* our life becomes the story *of* our life, because we do not so much tell stories, as stories tell us.

Her ancestors believed that true success starts within each of us. It is about being inner-led rather than striving for success as defined by the dictionary, or what common culture would have us believe it is: fame, power, money, having a big car, a great job, a good-looking partner, two-point-four children, and so on. While some of these may constitute success for some people, it does not have to be true for everyone.

Each generation in Parandin's family took the time to look internally to see what was true success for them; they then went and made this success a reality externally. This became the driving force for their own betterment, and that of the world around them. They recorded their successes, and what they had learnt, and handed this knowledge down to the next generation.

Parandin shared her story with me, but her family and her ancestors are a private people, and the story has been held sacred down the generations. She was happy for me to use her real name, but asked that her identity in all other aspects be protected, along with the actual details of their story. What she felt was most important was to share what she had learnt from her ancestors about how we can define true success for ourselves and make that into a reality.

Parandin's parents set up their hotel, as they believed that in so doing they were living out what true success was for them as individuals and as a family. The hotel was also meant to encourage and support all those who wanted true success in their own lives.

Everyone who worked at the hotel was there because they too wanted true success. During my time there I found that the staff always made themselves available, not just to talk to the guests, but to meet them and listen to what was going on for them. They were also very willing to share how they themselves were living lives of true success in the way they worked together at the hotel: they integrated all that the hotel stood for into their own lives.

The hotel itself was stunningly beautiful and very relaxing, and that, along with the staff, made it a real haven of support and encouragement for anyone who wanted to find out what a life of true success could be for them, regardless of the life they were living at the time. That said, it was all done in a way that was most unassuming. While there, I felt nourished, relaxed and peaceful. It was the perfect place to reflect on things. I particularly liked the library, which was a place of real serenity, where people could go to read an array of books written by some of the greatest writers of all time, as well as autobiographies and biographies of successful people. The suites in the hotel were all named after these successful people – as I would later come to discover.

Now, you may be thinking that such a hotel must market itself as a place to find success, but it does not! Most people who stay there have had the hotel recommended to them by other guests, who believed that they would be the better for having stayed there. Others are invited to stay by the hotel itself: people they like and admire, and who, they believe, would benefit from staying there. Some, like myself, end up there through a web of synchronicity or divine providence – call it what you like. Others just book in for a holiday, or because they are there on business, not realising what type of hotel it is. No matter how people end up there, and for whatever reason, the staff and the surroundings encourage them to discover what it would mean for them to be truly successful.

Everybody working at the hotel called it 'Hotel Falah': *falah* is the Arabic word for success. However, this is not the real name of the hotel. While they want guests to think of true success when thinking of this name, it was more important that, when their stay there is finished, they should let it go, and not get caught up with the idea of success the hotel stood for: to do so might well mean not focusing on what was true success for the person. So if you were hoping I would give you their details and tell you how to find it, then I am afraid you will be disappointed! If you are *meant* to stay there at some point, just trust that you will find your way there.

Parandin did not want people to get caught up with what the hotel sees as success. Instead, she wanted me to share my story, the conversations I had with her, and what I learnt about true success, in the hope that it would inspire, encourage and challenge you, the reader, to live your life of true success.

What follows is written to the best of my memory, and based on the few notes I took from our conversations, which spanned twenty-two hours. So whatever you do, wherever you are and no matter at what point you are in your life, if you are searching for your true success, this book is for you. You may be feeling:

- lost, with no real sense of what true success is for you or how it could be achieved in your life;
- angry and disappointed that the success you want for your life has evaded you to date;
- that you have been pursuing the wrong type of success for you, or even what others see as success for you;
- disheartened, believing that it is now too late in your life to achieve success; or
- that you are at an age where you are only now setting out in life, and want to know what it would be for you to live a life of true success.

Only now, none of these can be enough to stop you. The true success you want for your life can be made real; it really can. This is your life and your life alone; it is worth investing in it at every level. I wish you true success in every area of your life, in a way that is unique to you and that engages your heart at the deepest level. I encourage you to keep striving, even when you meet with disappointments along the way.

As I share this story of how I came to understand the meaning of true success for me through my travels and my conversations with Parandin, I hope it will inspire you to set out on your own unique journey, to discover what true success means to you.

PROLOGUE

At eight o'clock on Friday morning, 27 November 2015, I arrived in Singapore just as the river market was setting up for what would no doubt be a busy day. The streets were starting to fill up with people as I went to find my hotel.

It dawned on me that I had actually finished the Silk Road, one of the main parts of my journey from London to Sydney overland. It had been a dream of mine for years, and now I was at the end of that part of this adventure. Here I was in Singapore, having some time out to focus completely on the writing of my next book.

In truth I was in no hurry, as getting to the hotel meant having to sit down and write; and so far, the writing had not been going too well. In fact, I had parted ways with my agent and was feeling quite down about this. Yes, the book they wanted could be done, only something did not feel right: it was not the book I needed to write. Worse, I was having doubts about whether in fact I could write a book answering the question: what is true success?

So I was happy to mooch lazily around the wide, immaculate streets of Singapore, hopefully walking in the direction of my hotel, stopping off at the biggest fountain in the world: surely I could get some inspiration there. In this beautiful and pristine city, I must have looked a strange character, sitting there in the early-morning sunlight, shabbily dressed, unshaven, and with a backpack carrying all of my worldly possessions, including my tent, bedding and sleeping bag. Looking like I did, and attracting more attention than the fountain, it was time to move on and check into the hotel.

The hotel looked rustic and unusual from the outside, not at all in keeping with the striking modern buildings surrounding it. Only, it was startlingly different on the inside. I entered a truly impressive yet very homely lobby with a simple but beautiful chandelier, as the door was opened by the bell-boy, who welcomed me to Hotel Falah. He made it look as if they had shabbily dressed, rucksack-carrying people like me staying there all the time: for someone as young as he was, his professionalism was impressive. My having arrived on foot was in stark contrast to the very expensive cars pulling up outside, to either let people out to go into the hotel or to collect those who were leaving, but this in no way seemed to throw him.

The hotel radiated grace, style and simplicity, yet somehow offered real warmth as well. In a strange way – and this was something that I had never experienced before, and have never experienced since, in a hotel – there was something decidedly spiritual and peaceful about the place.

There was a smiling receptionist behind the front desk dealing with the person in front of her. Yet, as I walked to the reception desk, it appeared that at the first opportunity she made eye-contact with me, and gave a nod of acknowledgement that she had seen me, and that I would be looked after as soon as possible. All I could do was marvel at the beauty of the hotel and soak up the lovely atmosphere as I waited to check in. After a few moments, a gentleman – the manager, as I was later to find out – came from what I assumed was an office behind the reception desk. He smiled and said: 'You must be Michael. We have been expecting you. You are most welcome to Hotel Falah. I am Zafar. Please, let me check you in.'

I was not particularly surprised by the fact that he knew my name: sure, it could not be every day that an unshaven, rucksack-bearing person, dressed as I was, booked into their beautiful hotel. The most likely giveaway that he had been expecting me was the fact that I was there as a favour to a friend. As I signed the check-in forms, Zafar was apologising that my suite was not ready. He asked if it would be OK if I had some breakfast while they put the finishing touches to it. Having arrived so early and not having had any breakfast, I said I would be delighted to have some. All the while I wondered how it was going to be possible to pay for all this. My friend had told me that I would not have to pay the full price (as a favour to her from the hotel), but looking around me it still looked like it was going to be very expensive for me to stay here.

Once again the bell-boy was standing in front of me. Before I could say anything, he was offering to take my rucksack and leave it behind the desk while I went for breakfast. I explained that there was no need, as I was more than happy to carry it myself. Laughing, he said: 'Michael, it doesn't work like that in a top-of-the-line, luxury five-star boutique hotel like the one you are about to stay in: people get their bags carried for them here.'

I had to explain that having never stayed in such a hotel before, I was not used to the rules involved so, if it was OK with him, I would carry my own rucksack. We laughed together: sensing my discomfort in letting someone else carry my rucksack when I was perfectly able to do so myself, he left me to it. When I gave my rucksack to the receptionist at the desk, I asked her if it would be safe to leave it there, what with the clientele they must get in here. Then she, Zafar and the bell-boy all laughed along with me.

19 July, London, England

We christen it 'the Village'. Huge and unconventionally beautiful, it is going to be our home for the next nineteen weeks as we travel across Europe, Asia and South-east Asia to Singapore. (The last three weeks to Sydney from Kuala Lumpur will be by public transport and hired cars.) It really is happening, I think, as I board this overland vehicle at the Novotel Hotel car park in Hammersmith.

'The Village' is built to take everything in its stride: climbing mountains, crossing rivers and navigating everything from wet and marshy ground to hard, dry desert land, half-finished roads or, in some places, paths where the road has been washed away. It will shelter us from heat, cold, sandstorms and rain, and from the often overzealous curiosity as to where we have come from and where we are travelling to, from the many people we meet as we travel through so many different countries and cultures. But it doesn't 'do' technology: all it needs is a collection of maps, and a compass to transport us halfway around the world. After all, in order for GPS or sat-nav to work, you need a clear starting point and a precise destination: being sure of such information can be a real challenge when you are stuck in the desert or in some harsh environment halfway up, or indeed at the top of, a mountain. Yet it is always possible to find your way with a map and a compass.

Our group leader is Maria. She is Spanish, and proves to be a most efficient person and an all-round good woman, making sure our every need is met when it comes to accommodation, food and all else that is necessary to make a journey like this run as smoothly as possible. Our driver, Hans, is from South Africa. He also proves to be the go-to person to get issues and problems sorted out on the journey.

Our group of travellers is an eclectic mix of nine men and five women ranging in age from their early twenties to their mid-sixties. Nine are from England, one is from America and one is from Denmark – along with the group leader, from Spain, and the driver, from South

Africa. I am the sole Irish traveller. As 'the Village' leaves London, we tell each other why we have come on this journey.

Colin is a retired nurse who wants to do something new and exciting. Kevin is a science graduate just out of college, and wants to travel before starting work. Tim is a burnt-out college lecturer who has decided to take a much-needed career break. Billy has been made redundant from his job in banking, and is taking time out to think about what he wants to do next. He says he has no idea what that might be, except that it won't be banking! Liz, one of the youngest people in the group, doesn't know what to do with her life, and has left a job in retail and used her entire savings to come on the trip to figure it out. Wendy has been caring for her mother, who has just gone into a nursing home. She tells us that she is finally doing something for herself. There is also a young couple who want to go on the journey of a lifetime before getting married, settling down and having a family. Then there's Gerry, an avid traveller, who has always wanted to visit the 'Stans': Turkmenistan, Uzbekistan, Tajikistan, Kyrgyzstan and Kazakhstan — all places we are to visit during our journey along the Silk Road.

As the miles go by, we get along well together, and become a close-knit group. I become particular friends with two of them: Jim, who is our unofficial photographer and wants to make a career in this area on his return to England, and Emma, who is taking some time out from her profession in the hotel industry (and who passes on the favour that is to change my life). We are all very excited at the outset of the journey, but none of us can know that only eight out of the fourteen will make it all the way to Sydney.

Although we don't know it at this point, ahead of us is a twenty-two-week adventure driving across twenty-three countries — often run by dictators, some on the cusp of revolution, and many of them danger-ous to travel through for other reasons. Some days are dull drive-days on motorways; others are spent on roads that are little more than cart-tracks; others, off-road escapades across seemingly never-ending deserts.

There are thousands of miles to be travelled in severe temperatures. All the while 'the Village' is there to look after and protect us. Many personal challenges lie ahead of me, with an unexpected diversion that changes my life forever, in my quest to understand the meaning of true success.

CONVERSATION ONE
WHAT DOES TRUE SUCCESS MEAN TO YOU?

The bell-boy introduced himself as 'Lee' as he walked me to the dining area. He explained that while breakfast had just finished being served, there would be no problem with getting me something to eat. It was a short walk to the dining area, through the most beautiful yet simple glass corridor, with a glass roof. The pure sunlight coming through was nearly blinding, yet so warming: it was as if it was penetrating right through to my heart and soul; as if I was being led to receive nourishment at a much deeper, almost spiritual level.

From the moment I walked into Hotel Falah, I was completely aware of how beautiful the hotel really was, and this impression was not to change. I was taken aback by the stylish and light interior as we entered the dining area. A waitress greeted me as if she had been waiting for us to arrive; she introduced herself as 'Parandin'. Her big, welcoming smile immediately put me at ease in such surroundings. Having led me to a lovely booth, she handed me a breakfast menu. Even this was impressive in style, clearly set out on really fine paper and not offering too many options. (I have been told that this is often a real giveaway that all the food is not bought in but freshly prepared.) Having ordered pancakes and freshly squeezed orange juice, I sat back in the plush chair, wondering how much all this was going to cost, and thinking that there had better be a lot of writing done during the stay here, to make it all worthwhile!

I was disturbed from my thoughts by Parandin as she served my breakfast. Just as she had put down a glass of orange juice, she asked if I was looking forward to having some time out at the hotel to work on writing my book on true success. I was shocked: how did she know I was writing a book on true success?

Seeing the shock on my face, she smiled and told me that there was nothing to worry about: my friend, who had set me up in the hotel, had told her to expect me. With a twinkle in her eye, she said: 'Yes, sometimes having a friend who knows the waitress can mean a person gets looked after and booked into a hotel more quickly than anyone else!'

I could hear the honesty in her voice and see the sincerity in her face as she added that I was most welcome to the hotel and that I should relax and really enjoy my stay there. She explained that I was here as the guest of a friend, and that the friend had told her I was writing a book.

'So what is true success?' she said, with a smile. It was more a statement than a question. 'Is the greatest hunger in life for food, money, power, status, security, sex, or even love? For if it is, time and again people have achieved all of these things, in the belief that this would make their life one of success. Yet having achieved this success, they have wound up still feeling dissatisfied – indeed, often more dissatisfied then when they began.'

Never expecting to hear something like this over breakfast in a hotel, I sat there speechless. Before I could gather my breath and say anything, Parandin continued: 'It's great to have you here, Michael. Many people don't even ask what it would mean for them to be truly successful in their own life, let alone what it would mean to achieve success. Yet if you do ask yourself this question, and then answer it truthfully, it can more often than not lead to the truth of what you want for your life. If you take the time and effort to think through exactly what success means to you, it will bring more meaning into your life – which will help you spend time doing the things that are right for you, both now and in the future. This will make the success you wish for become a reality.'

She smiled at me and went on to explain: 'A lot of people have come to see success as being mainly concerned with the outer world and with something they have achieved, accumulated and now own. They believe that if they have more material wealth and possessions (like a bigger house, or a car, or a holiday home), they will feel happier, have a better view of themselves, and feel more secure in their life. While the conscious desire to feel secure is natural and important, and what they accumulate and own can lead them to feel more secure and successful, the truth is that the more they identify themselves with such external things and achievements – and everything that is impermanent – the more they tend to cling on to. Paradoxically, the more they have to lose, the greater their feelings of fear and insecurity may be.

'The world and society would have us believe this is success, and for the most part we have bought into this. Only for the self-leader, true success is inner-led. It means success across the board: personal, professional, and leaving a legacy. The pursuit of true success is based on living a life that is right for you, and one that does not transcend the rights of others or the natural laws of God.'

Before I could ask if she had read my last book about being a self-leader, Parandin said she had. I wondered, who was this girl working as a waitress in a Singapore hotel?

'It's the inner person who craves true success in life,' she continued. 'Regardless of how a life has been lived in the past, it is never too late to live a life of true success, one that is unique to each and every individual.'

I was still trying to get my head around what was happening here, and was about to ask her a question, when Parandin pointed out that the dictionary defines success as the achievement of something that is planned and attempted, such as as the attainment of wealth, position and honours.

'So, taking the dictionary's definition, to be successful you must achieve that which you have planned or attempted. (You are not considered a success just for trying, and making an effort!) Or you must attain wealth, high position or honours!'

Parandin looked at me and asked: 'Is this what you believe success to be, Michael?'

2 August, Gallipoli, Turkey

'You, the mothers, who sent their sons from faraway countries, wipe away your tears; your sons are now lying in our bosom and are in peace; after having lost their lives on this land, they have become our sons as well.'

I read this inscription on one of the walls as I walk around looking at all the names of those who lost their young lives here in Gallipoli.

Those who had died here had not all achieved wealth, fame or power. Does this mean they were failures? No, of course not, I think to myself. And yet, could you say that they had been successful? The Gallipoli campaign overall had not been a success. During World War I the first Australian troops from the Allied forces landed at Gallipoli in the early morning of 25 April 1915 with the aim of capturing it. Eight months of fighting ensued, with many casualties on both sides. The land campaign was subsequently abandoned, and the invasion force was withdrawn. It was considered to be a major Allied failure.

Looking at the individual gravestones, I realise that none of us know their reasons or motives for being here, the camaraderie they experienced with their fellow soldiers, and how they faced their end. If they truly believed in what they were fighting for, and acted on this, did that make them successful as individuals? Only they can know that, I think to myself – and who am I to judge them, anyway?

After leaving London, I had plenty of time to think and write about success while travelling through France, Luxembourg, Belgium, Germany, Austria, Hungary, Romania and Bulgaria.

But it is only here in Turkey, looking over the graveyards at Gallipoli, that I really feel grateful for the fact that I'm alive, and have at no time had to face what it is that they faced. Standing here reminds me that life is short and that surely true success cannot just be about things like money, fame or power, even though many of us are beguiled into believing it is. I realise that I still don't know exactly what success would mean to me – which also means that I feel no closer to writing my book! But I do know that I'm living at a great time in human history, and that I have no excuse for not coming to a real understanding of what true success is, and then going and living it.

Conversation Two
Is your health really your wealth?

Having finished my breakfast, and before I could respond to any of her questions – particularly whether I believed true success to be as defined by the dictionary – Parandin let me know that my suite was ready and that she was more than happy to bring me there. Having collected my rucksack from reception, we took the lift to the third floor. As she asked me about my travels so far, I had to concentrate, as all I could do was look at the palatial surroundings of the lift – wondering how a lift could be so beautiful. Sensing this, she said she could only hope that my suite would exceed my expectations. (This time, I did very much notice that she had not said 'room'; as I had never stayed in a suite before, my expectations had already been exceeded.) My next intake of breath was as we left the lift: the hallway leading to the suite was truly stunning. The floor was marble, with the most beautiful life-like patterns, and the walls were adorned with the most gorgeous embroidered sayings and quotes, which I found out later were made from silk from the Silk Road. On noticing my reaction, Parandin did not say anything but just let me take in my surroundings as we walked to the suite.

Parandin opened the door and let me go in first. Well, if the lobby was stunning, the dining area beautiful, the lift fabulous, the hallway magnificent, then the suite could only be described as spectacular. The room was like something out of a dream, with walls of windows; the furnishings looked as if the place had fallen right out of a magazine. She welcomed me to the O'Connell Suite (the significance of the suite's name only became apparent to me later on), and told me to go right ahead and make myself at home. She explained that each suite in the hotel had its own theme and design, and that the intention was for this one to have no frills and not be cluttered, to be elegant and accessible. The suite was super-minimalist, with clean lines that made the room feel very cosy and welcoming. Hotel Falah wanted guests to explore the island and all it had to offer, yet feel as if they were coming back home when they returned to their suite.

French doors led out to an expansive balcony with a gorgeous view of the Indian Ocean, which stretched as far as the eye could see. For a moment I just stood there, breathing in the salt air and watching the waves lap against the sand. I really was feeling a vivid sense of having come home, as though right now this was where I was meant to be, that I should take my stay here one day at a time and make the most of it. It was so very quiet and serene, away from the hustle and bustle of the city centre outside the hotel.

Coming back into the room, I noticed the super-king-size bed, the walk-in closet and dressing area, and the large, wall-mounted flat-screen television. The bathroom, in keeping with the suite, was big and beautiful, and contained a rain-shower, which I looked forward to using: I was now conscious that not only did I look scruffy but also that I must have the smell of someone who had been on the road for a long time!

There was also an off-room and separate living area, which included a very long sofa, a seating area and a gorgeous mahogany desk and chair: the perfect space for me to write my book,

Parandin said. All I could do was laugh nervously, for while I was here to work on the book, the only thing going through my head at that moment was how much all this was going to cost. Sensing my unease, she asked if everything was OK: was the suite to my liking? I replied that yes, the suite was very much to my liking, but I was nervous about how much it was going to cost me to stay here. Parandin explained that, as I was staying as the guest of a very good friend of the hotel, all charges were covered. Before I could respond, she went to leave, only stopping to ask if I would like some coffee served later, and if so, at what time. She said she did not want to be an interruption as I sat down to write about true success. (She seemed to be more interested in the question of what it was to live a life of true success than anything else!)

I said: 'That would be great. Would half past three be OK?' (I like to work in four-hour blocks of time when I'm writing.) I followed Parandin's reply of a simple 'Yes' with a simple 'Thank you'. It was all that I could think of in that moment: I was completely overwhelmed by all that had happened since my arrival in Singapore, especially at Hotel Falah. She replied: 'The guest does not need to thank the host, but the host the guest.' I recognised this as an Uzbekistan saying – a country I had travelled through on my journey along the Silk Road.

Just as she made to leave, she turned and asked: 'Michael, what do you believe is the most important thing for a person when it comes to true success?' I had spent so much time studying success, that it was easy for me to shoot straight back with my reply: 'Their health, of course. Sure, your health is your wealth, or so the saying goes.'

'But if our health was our wealth,' she responded, 'why is there such a rising use everywhere of antidepressants, alcohol, illegal drugs and painkillers? There is also the sad reality of how many people – especially young people – take their own lives every year. Now don't get me wrong, for there is an Arabian proverb that says: "He who has health, has hope; and he who has hope, has everything." So yes, it is often said that our health is our wealth. Yet, how true is it really?'

Parandin continued: 'It is often only when people get really sick and are facing death that they take up a hobby or lifelong interest they have always wanted to pursue. Why is it, do you think, that they then seem to live longer than they otherwise would have done?'

I nodded as she went on: 'We all know that when you care for your body, you also care for your mind; both are needed if you are to achieve the success you want in your life. Our body is the only instrument we have to experience life and make a contribution, but we always seem to be pushing ourselves and our bodies, even through the pain barrier, or when we are feeling unwell. After all, life can be tough, as we pursue a life of success that is true to us. So it is important that we allow ourselves to renew physically, mentally and emotionally, rather than spending so much of our energy and resources on external things – such as making ourselves look beautiful.'

Before she left, Parandin posed another question. 'So Michael, is it true for you then that your health is your wealth?'

As I sat there thinking about this, I noticed my rucksack sitting on the floor. Although I had been able to carry it myself, it was a relief to be able to shed the twenty-plus-kilogramme-weight from my shoulders. My whole life for being on the road was packed away inside the bulky, bulging bag. It contained everything that had been needed: clothes, pens, paper, laptop, first-aid kit, tent and sleeping bag. Every item had been chosen wisely, based on the principle of only bringing things we really needed. Each item had played its part in helping me deal with the many situations I had encountered, and the whole spectrum of temperatures I had experienced, from the desert heat of Iran to the cold mountains of China.

Having put the rucksack to one side and pushed back the thoughts of how it was I had ended up here with a book to write, I kicked off my boots, leaned back on the soft, brown leather armchair, put my feet up on the matching ottoman, and relaxed. Here I was practically living in luxury, and feeling so grateful for the chance to do so. I also felt really blessed to have been physically fit enough to make a trip like this, which in itself had been so full of wonderful experiences, and then to have the luck to meet someone on the trip who had enabled me to come and stay in this special hotel on such a beautiful island.

The only thing that kept me from really relaxing was the need to write. It was imperative for me to write – not because anyone was forcing me to, but because I felt I had to. This feeling would not go away. The need to write was only overridden by wanting to know who this lady was, with such thoughts and questions on the meaning of true success – somebody who was so free and easy in questioning me, and what I thought the true meaning of success was for the self-leader. I didn't have the time to reply to her question as to whether I agreed with the definition of success as set out by the dictionary: if I had, my answer would have been 'No'. For surely true success is unique to each and every one of us – as it no doubt was for all those young people who had lost their lives at Gallipoli.

But I still did not know what true success meant to me. I thought back over what Parandin had said about successful people, namely that they are prepared to take the necessary time out to discover what true success means to them, as they know they do not have to accept the traditional definition of success: notably wealth, fame and power. When looking to see what true success means to them, they turn inwards, knowing that they need to look to all areas where they want to see this success become a reality, such as their health, relationships, wealth, work, and leaving a legacy. They measure their success in relation to the person they are becoming during their time here on this earth, and not only what they are acquiring externally. In the end, they will define on their terms what true success is for them and their life. They also know that by doing this, they will encourage others to do the same.

Nobody else can say what true success is for each of us; only we can answer that for ourselves. So, did I still believe that my health was my wealth? Well, I thought, if you look after yourself, then you will perform better, and have a greater chance of achieving what you want. But so many of us do not take care of ourselves; I wondered why this was the case.

10 August, the border between Turkey and Iran

Just as we are walking across the border between Turkey and Iran, I notice a big sign saying:

THE FOLLOWING ARE NOT PERMITED IN OUR COUNTRY – NO ALCOHOL OR ILLEGAL DRUGS

We are well briefed as a group by Maria and Hans as to what can and cannot be taken across the border into Iran from Turkey. Following the Iranian Revolution of 1979, alcohol consumption is regulated under the Islamic legal term of hudud, *which means 'crimes against God'. Notwithstanding this, alcohol is the second most popular drug in Iran, after opiates.*

I'm about to enter a country that has been central to the Silk Road, and which I have long waited to visit for that reason. I have also been told that the people here are among some of the friendliest in the world; I am soon to discover that this is true.

So why then, I wonder, do so many people here (and all over the world) turn to alcohol, as well as both illegal and prescribed drugs. Why is it that we are prepared to sacrifice our health, both physically and mentally, just to get through the day, or for mere gratification?

I'm mulling over all of this during our long wait to cross the border into Iran, and start to talk to Wendy about it. She tells me that her decision to come on this journey is the single most important invest-ment she has made in her life: an investment in herself.

She tells me that she spent the best part of her life taking greater care of her family, friends, work and neighbours than of herself. While of course these were all worthy of her time and energy, this had often been to the detriment of her own wishes and desires. The deciding factor in her coming on the trip was the realisation that this way of living was having a negative impact on her health and well-being. She tells me that it's as though she was so busy driving, she didn't have time to stop for fuel.

I tell her that well-known saying about our health being our wealth – something we know all about in Ireland, because of our love of horses. She looks at me in astonishment.

I explain that if she were to visit any stud-farm in Ireland, or for that matter anywhere throughout the world, and look at the facilities and how the horses are treated, she would find top-of-the-range, pur- pose-built, heated stables, the best of food and individual diets. Now, if that is what is needed by way of investment for a two-million-euro horse, then how much is a human being worth, for we really are price- less pieces of work. Why is it that we don't invest in ourselves in the same way?

CONVERSATION THREE
DO YOU THINK YOU ARE WORTH IT?

As I lifted my head from the keyboard, Parandin was knocking at the door saying that my coffee was ready, and could she come in. I replied: 'Of course.' I could not wait to continue our conversations and find out about her and Hotel Falah.

'I have thought about all that you have talked about since we met,' I said. 'Yes, for the most part, people do accept that looking after their health is so important, yet so many just don't do it, including me.'

'Why do you think this is the case for you, Michael?' she asked.

I took a moment to think. 'I honestly go through phases of really looking after my health, exercising, eating properly, getting the right amount of sleep and rest, but what has stopped me from really carrying on and looking after my health is a need to tend to other commitments; or I get too busy and just don't have enough time to do all these things.'

Parandin said: 'People so often associate looking after their health and well-being with pain and discomfort – having to eat a proper diet, getting the right amount of sleep and rest, doing exercise, and so on. They often don't think that the time, effort and energy is worth it, for there is so much else they could be doing – like more work, and getting paid for it, eating and drinking for comfort, and so on. Only, Michael, what probably stops you, like most people, is none of these things. What stops you is that you start to feel good about yourself, and this is something most people struggle with: feeling good about themselves.

'So many start to take good care of their health but just can't keep it going. One of the reasons for this is so often that their own subconscious saboteur stops them being successful. Those core beliefs that tell them: "You are not worthy of success"; "You don't deserve to have things too good"; "Who are you to be feeling this good?"; "What's the point? It's all going to end in failure anyway – I won't lose weight (or whatever)." Knowing this is the case for you, Michael, you need to try to see that by looking after your health, you are investing in yourself at the very highest level; this is a real way of valuing yourself in terms of your own success and well-being.

'Probably the greatest benefit you will experience from looking after your health – including the physical, spiritual, mental and emotional aspects – will be the development of your "muscles of proactivity". Taking consistent actions based on the value of your own health and well-being, instead of reacting to all the forces that keep you from looking after it, will, first, enable you to believe in your own success and, second, give you the energy to achieve true success in all areas of your life.'

'What kind of actions?' I asked.

'Eating the right foods, getting enough rest and relaxation, and exercising on a regular basis. And keeping your mind sharp through reading broadly, journalling and meditating daily. It is also important to be aware of who you are spending time with, and to invest your effort and energy in people who support you.

'By being proactive about looking after yourself in all these areas, you will also tend to like yourself more. As opposed to a vicious circle, this becomes a positivity circle. And as you get caught up in this positivity circle, your own paradigm of yourself – your self-esteem, self-confidence and integrity – will be profoundly affected.'

'That's fascinating,' I said. 'Can we talk some more about this?'

'We will come back to it,' Parandin said. 'It is all wrapped up with self-esteem, which is vital to achieving success – success that is true and real. Feeling good about yourself starts with having a great relationship with yourself.'

She went on: 'The problem, Michael, is that so many of us just want to be accepted by the people who mean something to us – or to be part of the gang, the in-crowd. The difficulty with this is that we can end up living what others see as success for us. We are often more than happy to go along with that, as it will mean we are accepted, and stay part of the gang and the in-crowd. But we will never live to our fullest and reach our truest potential by letting someone else – be they parents, friends, family, neighbours or colleagues – define the meaning of our success.

'While many people take action because of social pressures, those that achieve true success often take action *despite* social pressures. Looking for others' approval, or not wanting to upset them, can often be the basis for the way in which many people make decisions in their own lives and relationships. If this has been the case for you, Michael, it will not be easy to change. Yet therein lies the challenge: to make those decisions and take those actions which will bring you to where you really want to go with your life. If you want to be truly successful, then you may have to be prepared to take actions which might not endear you to those people who matter in your life. Easily said, hard done!'

'Yes, it is hard,' I said. 'It reminds me of my friend Des, whom I met many years ago when I did a course about finding your purpose in life. Doing such a course was a big challenge for him. He came from a very conventional family and, like many of them, he had trained as an architect. He was very good at it and was making a nice living. Only he felt he was just going through the motions each day, putting in his time rather than enjoying his work.'

'Des had told me that his true passion was music: he was able to play quite a number of instruments. His dream was to play, teach and write music. Eventually he walked away from his career to follow his dream. His family, friends and colleagues thought he had gone mad, and in truth he felt a bit mad himself for exchanging such security for a dream that might not work out. Fortunately it did work out, and Des is now both playing and teaching music. While he does not make as much money as he did before, he says he would not swap it for the world.

Parandin agreed that this was an inspiring story, but then added: 'You can be sure, Michael, that Des paid quite a price for walking away from his circle of colleagues, friends and family in pursuit of the life he wanted to live. Often those achieving success that is true for them realise that they may have to reject from their life all the stuff that is inconsistent with the success they want. At times, this can include people. It sounds harsh, but it can't be helped; that is the way it is.

'You bring into your life everything that either supports or undermines who you are and what success you want to create, so choose wisely. Of course, this is a process – not a light-switch you can turn on or off. It's rough, and it can take a while. Tough decisions will have to be taken, and seen through. You may well have to make decisions which can have a major impact on the people in your life. It may mean moving away from people who no longer share the path you are now following, in pursuit of the success you desire.

'You must make decisions despite what others may think of you, and understand the need to be more emotionally committed to doing what you love than to being loved by others. Those who want true success that is unique to them often neither believe nor accept the traditional view of what society defines as success. They will not allow this to describe the success they want for their life and relationships if it is no longer a true indicator of what success is to them.'

'I understand what you mean,' I said. 'But it does sound a bit lonely. Are you saying that to be successful, you have do it all by yourself?'

'No,' said Parandin. 'What you need to do is to surround your-self with the right people, who will support and challenge you to grow, develop and achieve your full potential as an individual for your own benefit, as well as encourage you to make a difference in the wider world.' She went on: 'Having a supportive network or community around you will be an intrinsic part of achieving true success. As well as those who believe in you and cheer you on, you may need people with complementary skills and talents in all areas of your life.

'If such people are not in your life as you move forward, then you have to have the audacity to take the initiative in pursuit of the success you want, regardless. You have to really believe that as you move forward on this new path, the people who will stand by you and support you will come into your life. As I said, you may also have to walk away from those who don't want to support you in accomplishing what matters most to you. True friends will like you for your values and personality, not for your position and possessions.

'It is really about what you want for your life, what would be a real and meaningful understanding of success for you in all areas of your life. Ultimately it comes back to what we said earlier when we were talking about health, and whether you believe you are worthy of feeling good in yourself and about yourself.' She looked at me and asked: 'Do you believe you are worthy of success in your life, Michael, whatever that success means to you?'

I hesitated, and she went on: 'If this question makes you feel uncomfortable, it could be because that which deeply matters to you, and what you think the world and others expect of you, are two completely different things. Your enduring success must be constructed on a firm foundation of choices that only you can make, not on anybody else's idea of what success is for you. I invite you to ask yourself what really matters to you. What do you feel is the popular notion of success for you? Until you compare these two things and become consciously aware of what you believe to be success for you, you risk being motivated by what other people expect of you.

'And you may be afraid that if you pursue the success you want, and particular relationships, because they matter to you, you may not be as popular as you would like, or receive the recognition you wish for. Unfortunately, many people settle for popularity, acceptance and wealth over what truly matters to them. I encourage you to do the opposite, and pursue what is true for you.

'Similarly, I encourage you to value your true friends: those who always want what is best for you, and who cheer you on your way as you pursue success that is right and true for you. Sometimes these will be new people, who come into your life as you achieve the success you want; others may be old friends, who have always supported and believed in you. Remember, it is also important not to become so caught up in your own pursuit of a truly successful life that you let good, solid and true friendships slip by over the years. Make sure to give the true friend the time and effort their friendship deserves, and encourage them in pursuit of their own true success. The same goes for family members.'

It all seemed surreal. I had just spent the last four months, and more, studying and writing about success, and now here was Parandin asking the most basic of questions, yet getting to the centre of what true success and relationships were all about. Again, I wondered who she was. Yet before I could ask her, or get my head around what was happening here, she said she had a great deal of work to attend to, and that we would speak again that evening. She asked if it would be OK to meet in reception at eight o'clock, when we could go for dinner. I said I would be only too delighted to do so.

'So, see you at eight,' she said. With that, she was gone.

30 August, Samarkand, Uzbekistan

This evening I receive a call from a young man I met when we were travelling through Iran.

He had studied modern history (including the history of Ireland) at university, and we got on well. He was interested in my writing too, and wanted to stay in touch. When I was in Turkmenistan, he sent me an email asking for my Skype details, saying that he wanted to talk. But as he suspected that the hotel rooms of Westerners staying in Turkmenistan were often bugged, he asked if it would be possible to contact me when I was in Uzbekistan, the next country we were to visit. By this point, I am most intrigued to find out what he wants to talk about without being overheard.

During the phone call he tells me that he is gay – which is against the law in Iran. Yet as he talks, there is no sense of self-pity, or of him having been given a raw deal in life for having been born in a country where you cannot be openly gay. In fact, the opposite is the case. He explains that in accepting his own sexuality, he has come to a greater understanding of himself, and is now so much more compassionate, towards both himself and his fellow human beings.

'I'm choosing to live my life to the full, Michael,' he says. 'I'm trusting that I'll find a partner when the right time comes. Although I realise that this may also mean I won't necessarily have one exclusive relationship in my life, that is OK.'

'How do your family and friends feel about that?' I ask.

'Oh, they want me to be married and have children and are doing all they can to try to make this happen!' he says, with a sigh.

We talk about how life can be so hard and tiring when you try to please everyone. I tell him the story about the man and his son who were bringing their ass (in Ireland, an ass is another word for donkey) to the fair. The man was walking with the donkey, and his son was up on the animal's back. A passerby said: 'Isn't it a disgrace to see that poor man walking, and the young fellow up on the donkey having an easy time. He should walk, and let his poor father have a rest.' So the boy dismounted and the father took his place. A mile later they met another man, who said: 'Isn't it a disgrace to have that boy walking while his father takes it easy. You should both get up on the donkey's back.' They duly did so, but a short time later they met an enraged woman, who screamed: 'How cruel it is to have two healthy men up on that poor donkey's back! The two of you should get down and carry the donkey.' Again they did as they were told. But as they walked over a bridge, the donkey fell into the river and drowned. The moral is that if you are trying to please everyone, you might as well kiss your ass goodbye!

He laughs and says he has accepted that if he wants to have a successful relationship, it is likely to be without the support and approval of others. Although he struggles with this sometimes, he also knows how important it is to be true to himself. He says this is about loving himself, and choosing what is the very best for him.

After the call ends, I think about my book. I'm lucky that I have this opportunity to travel and take time out to write it, and also have the support of my family, friends and fellow travellers.

But, I wonder, do I have that support from myself? Do I believe I'm worthy of writing a book that feels true to me?

Conversation Four
How much is enough?

I closed my computer down, having spent the last four hours sitting in the very comfortable leather chair at the beautiful mahogany desk in my suite, reflecting on what Parandin had asked me about relationships, and the need to be accepted. Then I looked at the clock and realised it was eight o'clock, and I was supposed to be meeting her in reception.

She was there at the front desk, talking and laughing with the receptionist. On seeing me, she beckoned me to join them. She introduced me to Natalya, and we talked about where we could go to eat. Having agreed on the Butchers Club – we both wanted burgers – we bid Natalya farewell.

Parandin asked if it was OK for us to walk to the restaurant, as she wanted to show me Read Bridge at Clarke Quay. In the past, labourers and those working on the Singapore river used to gather at the bridge to listen to stories and storytellers. She hoped that this would inspire me in my writing.

As we walked, she told me that she was delighted that I had got to travel the Silk Road, as it had really made her father the person he was. His family originally made their living – and wealth – from transporting cargo on the Silk Road but, over time, as the development of the railways drastically cut down journey times, they invested in transporting their goods and cargo by rail. The family moved into construction after the breakup of the Soviet Union; as travel restrictions eased, they also became involved with tourism. This was something her father was particularly interested in, as it allowed him to travel extensively and work with people from many different cultures and religions. Through travelling, he was able to learn many foreign languages and gain an insight into different political systems and economic ideas. He then fed back into his own family and their businesses all that he had learnt from his travels, and from the many business and personal contacts he had built up. But most important of all for him was that, while travelling the Silk Road, he had met the woman who was to become his wife, and give the couple their daughter, Parandin. She proudly declared that her name meant 'silk'.

She went on to tell me that her father was a Muslim Tatar, originally from Turkey, with Iranian roots; her mother was an Orthodox Christian whose family came from Russia, and had ended up in Uzbekistan having travelled along the Silk Road too. Their marriage was frowned upon, yet in truth it reflected perhaps a thousand years of Silk Road history.

Her parents' hotel was where Parandin was educated and now worked. Before I could stop myself, it was out of my mouth: 'But you are a waitress! Not that there is anything wrong with working as a waitress – only your parents do own the hotel.'

'Yes,' she said, 'they do, and they want the hotel to be something special, something different – something that holds up a reflection to modern life, to those who are striving for what society and the world consider to be success. The hotel is about giving these people a new perspective on what true success really is.'

Sadly her father had died in an air accident, and it was now only her mother who ran the hotel – which would one day become Parandin's, if she so wished. Her parents both wanted her not only to learn all the workings of the hotel, but also, in tandem, understand what it was that they, as a family, wanted the hotel to reflect when it came to living a life of true success.

She said that it had been less than a year since her father's death, and that the loss was still quite raw for her. I said I could see this, and that I felt for her, as my own father was dead too.

She thanked me, and went on to say that in essence, she would work her way up the ladder to one day owning the hotel, if she so wished. Having first worked in the kitchen, cleaning pots and pans, she then went to work in housekeeping, moving on to work in stocks and provisions. After working alongside the receptionists, she was now in the restaurant and bar collecting glasses, and serving food and drinks. She was just about to become the assistant manager; having worked in this position for a few years, she would travel overseas to gain more experience in the hotel industry before returning to the hotel as general manager – if she so wished.

In creating a successful hotel, her family had also had to face challenges and difficulties, but Parandin said that she did not want to share the details of that journey, as what constitutes true success for one person does not have any bearing on what constitutes true success for another. She believed that we all have to follow our own path to success.

'I understand what you mean,' I said, 'but I do still find it inspiring to look at other "successful people", both known to the public, and others that are only known to us within our own lives; it gives me hope, and encourages me on my way.'

I told her that I really admire the following people, and that they have all inspired me in some way:

Albert Einstein He was not able to speak until he was four years of age, and his teachers said he would 'never amount to much'.

Michael Jordan He was initially cut from his high school basketball team for 'not being good enough'.

Walt Disney He was fired from a newspaper for 'lacking imagination' and 'having no original ideas'.

Oprah Winfrey She was demoted from her job as a news anchor because she 'was not fit for television'.

The Beatles They were rejected by Decca Recording Studios because 'We don't like their sound: they have no future in showbusiness'.

Parandin smiled and said she could see how I would find these people and their stories uplifting and inspiring; she too had many people she admired. I said that I also admired Steve Jobs and the way in which he made a comeback even after being unceremoniously removed from Apple, which he had founded. Although, I added, I was not sure he was right to go back to the company: maybe he had much more to offer the world. Plus, I believed that going back to Apple may have had a detrimental effect on his health, and may have contributed to his early death.

Parandin said: 'I'm delighted you mentioned Steve Jobs. For there is no doubt the man was gifted; but he was human too, like all those you have mentioned. Everyone has their flaws, and so we need not sanctify them. We also need to be gentle with ourselves when we fall short in living up to our own standards, and be empathetic towards others when they fall short in living lives of true success.'

She asked if I had noticed that many of the suites in the hotel had been named after successful people. Other than my own suite, the O'Connell Suite (the significance of which hadn't been apparent to me at the time of being let into the suite), I had not! They had named the suites after these people not only because they admired and respected them, but also because they wanted guests to reflect on the great personal costs that are often involved in attaining true success. Many of the people they admired had had to endure challenges, disappointments and setbacks in order to achieve success that was true to them, and live as they wanted to live. While ultimately we cannot compare our lives directly to theirs, because each and every one of us should follow our own path, we can follow their example, in order to understand what constitutes our own true success.

Just as we got to Clarke Quay and Read Bridge, the area of stories and storytellers, Parandin turned to me. 'I will tell you the truth, Michael,' she began with a heavy sigh, as if preparing herself for the dramatic story she was about to tell. 'All we have discussed, and will discuss further, about true success, and all the questions I have asked, were written in the secret books of my family's tree. And you know that old men and women – our grandfathers and grandmothers, and their grandfathers and grandmothers – never lie.'

As she talked and shared her story, her calmness and knowledge made her appear much older than she was. Her family were private people, who were completely committed to knowing what it was to live a life of true success for each and every one of them. Down through the generations, this was only shared and known among them. While there was no formal initiation, or secret rites of passage, to both knowing, and then achieving, true success, they did work together to see each and every member of the family achieve success. This was the case when they built

Hotel Falah. First, they spent two years reflecting internally, and planning the project. It took another four years to develop and build the hotel. Now they wanted to share the knowledge and traditions of the secret books in terms of the décor and the services they were providing to their guests, and the way in which their staff worked together as a team. This is what they had been doing for eight years, since the hotel opened.

In essence, Parandin's family had taken the sacred books and all that was written in them – which, Parandin said, was beyond ordinary understanding and in itself quite mysterious. Until now, they had never shared what was in these secret books. Although she did not wish me to reveal these details (in order to respect the privacy of her ancestors), she believed in the information contained in the sacred books so much that she wanted me to share the general wisdom that emerged from them. She had distilled this information into a set of questions that, if answered truthfully, can assist everyone in deciding what true success means to them and their life. She went on to say that honesty and fair dealing were very much what her people were about. This had often led to great success for them.

Parandin then looked me in the eye and said: 'While you are staying at Hotel Falah, I will continue to share all these questions with you. Your challenge is to tell this story and share these questions with the wider world. Are you happy to do that?'

Despite the fact that I still felt confused and surprised, and had lots of questions going round in my head, I looked at her and said: 'Yes, of course I am.'

We took our seats in the restaurant. After we had ordered, the first words out of Parandin's mouth were: 'What do you think is the secret to making money?' She did not expect an answer. (She really was good with these rhetorical questions!)

'You might be glad to hear that there isn't a hidden secret to making money. It is a skill that can be learned and developed. Famous entrepreneurs are not born under a lucky star that gives them the ability to make money. There's no magic pill, no instant transformation, no miracle. People who are successful at making money are just like the rest of us. The only difference is that they have taken the time to learn about making money, about savings, investments and pensions. They know how best to plan their way to a solid financial future, so that they have the financial resources to live the successful life they want to live. They have decided how much is enough for them to achieve this. I know, Michael, for we have met them all at the hotel, whether their wealth was self-made or inherited.

'So, when it comes to money, Michael, how much is enough for you?' Before I could answer, she continued, 'If, for you, success is to be financially rich, how much do you need in order to be so? If you were to have this amount of money, what would you do with it? What are the chances of you accumuluating this amount of money? If you didn't achieve this amount, are you saying that you aren't successful, and won't get to live a good, enjoyable and successful life?'

Parandin's question took me right back to when I was training to be a monk in Ireland. During these years, I took the religious vow of poverty (as well as the vows of chastity and obedience). This was a public vow, and was binding in Church law.

The vow was not about being poor; it was about sharing that which you had, including your money and all your material resources. It was about having just enough to maintain your physical, emotional and spiritual health. In truth, my conduct, practices and views on money have not changed much since then. Although I fully accept that, like all people, I need a certain amount of money to be able to live, and to give me some security, as well as having enough for the enjoyable things in life, like travelling, there is only so much that I actually need.

She went on: 'Regardless of how much we think we need to be rich, whether we are aware of it or not, I think we all have an amount of money in our head that we're comfortable having. When you have more than that at your disposal, you find a way of getting rid of it: you go on a shopping spree, change the car, buy some new furniture or treat your friends to lunch. You may not realise it, but money burns a hole in your pocket when it is above the level of your financial comfort-zone. You're uncomfortable with that much money, and you spend your way right back to your subconsciously chosen 'number'. Conversely, if your bank balance falls below this level, you also become uncomfortable, as you feel exposed. You find that you redouble your efforts to earn more, and to save, whenever your bank balance goes below this "number".

'We all have a comfort-zone: the upper and lower limits are defined by our self-image. It is "like us" to operate within this zone. If we start having more or less than the limits of our comfort-zone, we become troubled, and tend to either save or spend our way back to the comfort-zone. Our self-image will provide us with extra power to improve, until we are back within the zone.'

Parandin continued: 'Your self-image makes you act like you, Michael. It keeps you within your comfort-zone. If you are below your zone, your self-image makes you uncomfortable, and turns up your power until you are within the zone. Likewise, if you are above your zone, the self-image will cut your power, dropping you back within your zone. As long as you "act like you", the self-image is content and does not interfere. To change the level of success you want in all areas of your life, including wealth, you must change your self-image and raise your comfort-zone.'

As we finished our meal and were getting ready to return to the hotel, Parandin said that we would talk about this again. Now, however, she had a question for me: 'If being rich means you are successful, what does being rich really mean?'

8 September, bush-camp, Tajikistan-Afghanistan border

Sitting here with the group after dinner overlooking the Pamir river; it's a truly spectacular sight.

The landscape is wild and rocky. A clear, fast-flowing river slices its way effortlessly through the dense mountain range, creating a border between us, camping on the banks in Tajikistan, and Afghanistan on the other side. We can see remote Afghan villages, as a myriad of stars light up the sky.

We are here for one night and have an early start. The cruising speed of 'the Village' is only about fifty miles (eighty kilometres) per hour, and in any case we couldn't go any faster on these challenging mountain roads.

For a while we all sit in silence, breathing in the cold, clear mountain air, no doubt all wondering how the people in those remote villages can possibly eke out a living, let alone have any kind of quality of life, in such a desolate place. Then Colin says that it reminds him of the following story.

A father took his daughter on a trip to the countryside, to show her how the poor live. They spent a day and night on the farm of an extremely poor family. When they came back from the journey, the father asked his daughter: 'Well daughter, how was the trip?' to which the daughter replied: 'Great, dad, really great.'

'So now, daughter, you know how it is poor people live.' The daughter agreed that she did. The father then asked her to tell him what she had learnt from their trip. The daughter gave the following answer: 'I got to see that we have one dog and they have two. We have a swimming pool; they have a river, which ends behind the horizon. We have lights imported from a foreign country, and they have the stars. Our garden is surrounded by a fence; they've got endless fields.' The father

was speechless, and after a moment of silence, his daughter went on to say: 'Thank you, father, for showing me how poor we are.'

Now, lying here in my tent, I think about Colin's story and ask myself if I feel wealthy . . . truly wealthy. I'm camping on the side of a mountain in the freezing cold on the Afghanistan border, yet I feel so peaceful and safe. I think about life and all that I have: good health, hobbies, the chance to make a life by sharing my own unique gifts and talents with the world. Only this is a material world. We need money to function in it. Our culture encourages us to acquire everything now, *whether we need it or not. In this moment I feel that I have everything I need (rather than everything I may believe I want). I wonder, is this true wealth?*

Conversation Five
Do you love the work you do?

As we returned from the restaurant and our walk to Read Bridge, Parandin asked me what I thought of Hotel Falah. I told her it was something special – really amazing – and that I was very grateful to be staying there. She explained that it was her father's intention that the hotel should welcome all (regardless of who could pay or not), and that its guests should be a reflection of the cross-culture of the Silk Road and all those who travelled on it, made their living or wealth from it (as he had), or lived along it. Hotel Falah was to be a place of real and true success for her parents (and for Parandin too, if she so wished in the future). It was to be a place of mutual respect and greeting, hospitality, acceptance and embrace, regardless of how those who stayed there viewed success. He wanted the hotel to reflect true success as it was lived by those he admired, not as it was defined by common culture or the dictionary. She joked that as I had not yet noticed who the suites were named after, I should go and look at the ones on my floor.

On getting back to the hotel, I was delighted when she said, as we bid goodnight, that she would be more than happy to serve breakfast in my suite at seven o'clock the next morning so that we could continue our discussions. With that, once again, she was gone.

Although I had noticed the silk embroidered sayings on my way to the O'Connell Suite when checking in, the significance of the name had been lost on me. As I walked down the corridor to my suite, it struck me straight away who the suites were named after. The first one was the Ali Suite (named after Muhammad Ali, Muslim), then the Su Suite (named after Mother Su: Aung San Suu Kyi, Buddhist) followed by the Gandhi Suite (Mahatma Gandhi, Hindu), the Frank Suite (Anne Frank, the young Holocaust victim and diarist, Jewish), the Dawkins Suite (Richard Dawkins, atheist), the Tutu Suite (Bishop Desmond Tutu, Christian), the Stevens Suite (Yusuf Islam, formerly Cat Stevens, Muslim) the Hanh Suite (Thich Nhat Hanh, a Buddhist monk), the Indira Suite (Indira Gandhi, Hindu), the Frankl Suite (Viktor Frankl, a neurologist, psychiatrist and Holocaust survivor, Jewish) and the Hawking Suite (Stephen Hawking, agnostic). My own suite was named after Daniel O'Connell, who was a Christian, from Ireland. The suites were named after people from all different religions and none, who had pursued success very much on their own terms, and often through considerable hardship. Many had followed an unconventional path, but they had done so in a way that was true and meaningful for them.

I woke early the next morning having had a really good, deep sleep. There may have been a rain-shower in the bathroom, but I was not going to miss the chance of having a real bath when such a big one was available – plus, the rest of the gang on the trip would never have forgiven me if I hadn't taken that particular opportunity, for we had few chances of having a bath while on the road! Closing my eyes, and thinking about what Parandin and I had spoken about the day before, I slowly slipped lower into the bathtub.

Just as I finished dressing, there was a knock on the door at exactly seven o'clock. It was Parandin, bearing a tray with breakfast.

She set down the tray and, before I could answer her question from last night about how much is enough when it comes to wealth and money, she started with another question. So it was going to be a working breakfast.

'Do you enjoy your job, Michael? Do you love the work you do?' For the most part, she did not expect me to answer her questions immediately. It was not that she did not care about my answers; she was interested in them, but she wanted me to think about and reflect on them, so as to answer them properly. Her questions were all those the self-leader asks of themselves on an ongoing basis, as they set out to achieve the life they need to live for it to be one of true success for them.

'It is often said,' Parandin continued, 'that if you want to achieve true success in your work, then loving what you do will assist you in getting there. For you to love your work, it must reach into your heart in a personal way, so as to unlock all you have to give. "Love" is a big word. So, while you need to love what you want to do and achieve, you do not have to love all of it all of the time: in fact, it is highly unlikely that you will. To love most of it most of the time is more than enough. Every job can be tough, and there will be times when it will leave you tired, stressed out and complaining about it, regardless of how much you love it. Even people like my father and mother, who had their dream job of running their own hotel, had parts they didn't enjoy, and maybe even hated doing some days. That's just work and life.

'If you want to have success in your work, you need to figure out as best you can what you love to do and are strong at, then go and put these strengths to work. You are already doing this, Michael. You found where your strengths lie and what you love to do. What you do, seems to come so naturally to you: it's like you're not trying when you do it. This is what happens when you do something you enjoy, and which therefore holds your attention. You wrote about all these things in your book on self-leadership: how people need to consider which activities come naturally to them, where they feel 'in the flow' and are able to focus easily, just as you did. If they can discover what these things are, they can be pretty sure this will lead to them achieving success in their work.

'The truth is that, as you focus on doing the work you love, you will have more energy and enthusiasm to achieve the success you want. Likewise, your willingness to become very good at what you love to do – for its own sake – is crucial to success. In a strange way, for those who stay true to what they love to do, things actually have a knack of turning out better than they imagined they would.'

She went on: 'It comes back to self-esteem, Michael. As we have said before, you need to feel you are worthy of the success you want. Successful people don't obsess over what others may think about them and their work. They are more concerned with doing what they love, than with being loved. They have found success that lasts because they have pursued that which matters to them – often at the cost of popularity or recognition. Most people do the opposite: they do things because of their need for approval, popularity or recognition, rather than pursuing what matters to them.

'Having discovered your strengths, it is very important that you put these to use in pursuit of doing what you love to do. Believe in yourself and your talents; discover what it is that you are passionate about; pursue your dreams, and do not worry about getting a "good job". Decide to do only what it is you love to do.'

I said that I believed that every decision we make in life comes from either a place of fear or a place of love. I believed that my decision to write a book about the meaning of true success had come from a place of love. Yes, for a while I did give in to fear, and wrote about success in the way my agent wanted me to, even though I knew that this did not sit right with me. I feared that I was letting him down and that in all probability I was blowing a publishing deal, which was most likely going to pay for this trip, and the journey I was on. It really was a case of play it safe and give the agent what he wanted, or take a risk to believe in my own self-worth and use my talent for writing a book on a subject about which I am passionate. Should I choose to pursue one of my dreams, and write about what true success means to me, rather than let the fear win and give in, for the chance of receiving a pay cheque?

Parandin agreed. 'Really successful people focus on being good at what is meaningful to them, doing things because they matter, and not just doing whatever comes along. They do this despite pressure from society and the risk of being unpopular. They seek out what it is they love to do, and then go and do it. Real success for them is making a difference and creating a lasting impact; it does not mean always achieving fame, money or power. Equally, making a difference in this great world of ours and making money too is OK: it doesn't have to be a case of either one or the other. So, having discovered what you love to do, the challenge is to go and do it!'

Talking about work, she said, she needed to get on with hers, and leave me to get on with my writing. As she reached the door, she turned to ask if I would be free to go for lunch, as she wanted to show me somewhere else here in Singapore that would be of interest to me as an Irishman.

'And we still have much more to talk about.' I did not doubt it!

21 September, Kyrgyzstan-Kazakhstan border crossing

It is his smile and enthusiasm that is most infectious, as he asks us for our passports and to fill out the documentation which will allow us enter Kazakhstan. He is by far the friendliest, most courteous and welcoming border-crossing official we have yet dealt with. He really is the exception: unlike most of the others we have come across, he isn't looking for a bribe.

He introduces himself as 'Marat' and goes on to tell us, in broken English, that he loves his job, as he gets to welcome people to 'his' beautiful country – particularly those who have never been to Kazakhstan before. He loves making people's entry to his country as smooth as possible.

'Do you never have bad days?' one of our group quips. He smiles and says that he doesn't love it when there is a visa or passport issue prohibiting a person from entering, and he has to fine them or, worse, turn them back. But he says it is a great feeling when he can resolve the situation to everyone's satisfaction. 'When that happens, I feel as though I'm doing more than just making a living,' he adds. We are happy that this is a good day for Marat: he is able to welcome our entire group to 'his' country; thankfully, there are no problems with any of our documents or passports.

As we leave the border crossing and walk back towards 'the Village', we are all smiling and praising Marat. One of our group, Tim, says to me that Marat has a tough job, but clearly always does his best, regardless of the circumstances with which he has to deal.

He goes on to say that the main reason he came on this journey is because he has burnt himself out. 'I was so busy striving to make a living that I had forgotten how to live life itself.' He laughs and adds: 'I'm not sure I'll ever love my job the way Marat does, but he has reminded me that there are many elements of my job that I do love.'

Tim is an accountancy lecturer and says that he particularly enjoys interacting with his students and seeing them grow and develop, as well as doing research to keep up with the latest trends and developments in his field. He says that lately, though, he has found himself focusing on all the areas of work he struggles with, like dealing with the inner politics of the university, the ever-growing amount of paperwork, and the bureaucracy that he endures on a daily basis.

'Would you like to do something different?' I ask him. He is silent for a moment and then says, 'No, I wouldn't. I simply need to accept that there are some aspects of my job that I will never really enjoy, but they don't have to detract from those areas I really love.'

He adds: 'Coming on this trip has also reminded me to value myself and to have more fun and adventure in my life. These things used to be important to me, but somewhere along the way I have forgotten that. I need to be mindful and proactive about taking the time to do what I love to do outside of work as well.'

Tim speaks with such certainty, and we look at each other, by way of acknowledging that he has just said something very important, and that he is going to make this happen when he returns home.

As we board 'the Village', I realise that many of us are making inner journeys, as well as this outer one.

CONVERSATION SIX
WHAT IS YOUR LEGACY GOING TO BE?

It was lunchtime already. Meeting her in reception, Parandin wasted no time in saying, as she had in the morning, that she wanted to show me somewhere that would be of interest to me as an Irishman.

My whole experience to date in Hotel Falah had been both surreal and at the same time spell-binding; this was no different. All I could do was follow Parandin out of the hotel and onto the street. I struggled to make any logical sense of all that was going on here. For all that we had spoken about so far in our short time together, I had a sense that this was going to be something special.

The next thing I knew, we were standing in front of Coleman Bridge, which crosses the Singapore river, and Parandin was explaining that the bridge was built in 1840 to join Old Bridge Road and Hill Street. It was designed by, and named after, George Drumgoole Coleman, an Irishman who was Singapore's first architect. She said that it was also referred to as the 'New Bridge'. 'So when we have finished our time together, Michael, let our conversations, the questions asked of you, and your answering of them, become a "new bridge" from what common culture and the dictionary would have us believe is success to what is real, true success, defined internally, and not just in terms of acquiring, or having, material success.'

I was stunned: here she was, asking me to share all that we had spoken of and all that she had been taught about success down through the ages. Yet before I could respond, she was taking me by the arm and leading me up Coleman Street and into one of the local restaurants. After we had taken our seats and ordered our food, she picked up from where she had finished that morning, as she served breakfast in my room.

'Michael, there is an old Greek proverb that says: a society grows when old men plant trees whose shade they will never see.' I replied that I liked the proverb.

'That is the power of legacy,' she continued. 'When people seriously undertake to identify what true success means to them in their work and life, it becomes important to them that it is a reflection of the person they are, and the life they want to lead. They become reverent, and start to think in larger terms than just today and tomorrow. Whether they're running a household, a company or a country, those who want to achieve great success also want to leave a legacy. They recognise that although this type of success begins with them, it does not end with them. Such success not only contributes to their own personal growth, but also helps create a better world for others, even after they have gone.

'They understand and accept that the greatest things they have done, and the legacy they will be proudest to leave, is what they did to help others. Nobody will care about how much money they made, what car they drove, or what prizes they won. They understand that it will not be possible to take anything of monetary value with them when they die. They won't wait until they are on their deathbed to realise that what really mattered most was the true relationships they had, and the actions they took to improve the lot of others.

'Michael, the most powerful motivator in the world is to have a purpose: to set out a definition of the true success you want for your life, in which you can invest every ounce of yourself: a purpose that will become your driving force, your raison d'être. Those who are intent on living a life of true success focus too on leaving a footprint and making a difference for having lived. They make sure to live a life of purpose – a purpose in pursuit of leaving this world a better place for having had them in it. Humans, by their nature, seek purpose: a cause that is greater and more enduring than themselves. People leave well-paying jobs for purpose-driven ones. They ask themselves: what do I hold most sacred; what can I pass on to others?'

I tell Parandin that she has reminded me of someone I know back home. Since 2010, I have been a guest teacher at a university in Germany for their International Project Week, which is run once a year for the students who are studying social work, social administration, international business and engineering. I have become very good friends with one of the lecturers there.

Her parents were originally from East Germany but fled after World War II, leaving behind many family members. She grew up in West Germany and made a good life for herself and her family by running her own international consultancy business. However, she never forgot those who had been left behind; when the Berlin Wall came down in 1989, she and her husband sat down and discussed what they could do to support the integration of East and West Germany. They decided they wanted to give something back to those less fortunate than themselves, and allow their lives to take on a new purpose, where they shared all the knowledge, skills, expertise and contacts they had built up over their years in business. Although she could easily have gained a professorship at a well-known university, she chose instead to move to this little-known university. It is a decision she has never regretted, as the university has gone from strength to strength over the years because of people like her and her husband, who made the decision to give up their comfortable lives so they could make a difference.

Parandin says this is a very inspiring story, and agrees that the key to any form of success, and particularly great success, is 'to know the way, and then go the way'. What is special about those who want true success is that they will not settle for less. She says, 'You too can be like this, in your own way, regardless of what has gone before, or what is in your life at this time.

'If this is to be the case, then there really is a need to work at knowing yourself well enough, to recognise where and how it is you can have your greatest possible impact on life, whatever shape, form or size this takes. You have the choice to embrace a journey that is meaningful to you, integrating your personal and professional life, in ways that can make a lasting difference.'

She went on: 'You need to ask yourself the following question: what unique gifts do I have to share, and how can I use this uniqueness to achieve the success that I want, and to leave a legacy long after I have departed from this world? It's all about discovering who you are and what it is you do, and then deciding how and where you can use this to make the greatest impact, and for whom. So if you are a painter, paint. If you are a musician, compose music. Michael, you are a writer and a storyteller, so write, and tell this story.

'Yes, these are big ideas, and maybe the legacy for most people is to have lived a life of true success doing what they loved to do, just giving themselves completely to that which they want to pursue, regardless of the personal cost or consequences. I don't mean the big fanfare-type success that is so often presented on television or written about in the newspapers, but success on your own level – success that is meaningful to you, and which touches those you come into contact with, whether they are aware of it or not.'

Finally, with a twinkle in her eye, she said: 'Maybe, Michael, the writing and telling of this story is going to be your legacy.'

2 October, bush-camp, Turpan, China

'Have you ever been really scared during the journey so far?' asks Liz, as we are having dinner in our camp in one of the lowest-lying areas in China.

'Yes,' I reply immediately. 'When we were driving along the Pamir Highway at nearly five thousand metres above sea level, I was really scared.'

'Me too,' she says, laughing.

The truth is, we were all scared, but we had chosen to take the risk. The Pamir Highway is officially called 'M41', and is the only continuous route through the Pamir Mountains. It is part of the ancient Silk Road and passes through Afghanistan, Uzbekistan, Tajikistan and Kyrgyzstan; it is the second highest international highway in terms of altitude.

I think back to the journey and wonder what would have happened if it had all gone wrong as we drove along the stretch sometimes known as 'the Road from Hell' – as it is heavily damaged in places because of erosion, earthquakes, landslides and avalanches. It was certainly breathtaking in every sense of the word: there were times when we suffered from serious altitude sickness, as some sections of the road have a notorious lack of oxygen. Evidence of the highway's fearsome reputation was plain to see as you looked down from nearly five thousand metres above sea level to the debris of those cars, trucks and buses that had slipped over the edge. One mistake could have been fatal: there was no barrier between the road and the cliff-edge.

'Even though I felt scared, I wouldn't have swapped it for anything in the world,' says Liz. 'I gave up my job to come on this trip. My family thought I was mad to do it, and at the time it felt like a big deal, but now, having made it this far on the trip, I feel like I can do anything with my life. I want to follow my dreams and inspire others

to do the same. You know the saying: "Magic happens out of your com-fort-zone"? Well, I really believe that now.'

As the evening draws on, I think about all this, and suddenly writ-ing my book, the one that is really inside me, definitely feels doable, dare I say easy!. But most of all, it feels essential.

CONVERSATION SEVEN
WHAT IS STOPPING YOU?

After lunch, Parandin and I walked back to the hotel in silence, allowing time and space for me to think about what we had discussed about leaving a legacy. Yet, all the while this was going on in my head, there was one overriding thought that would just not go away. On reaching the hotel, the question had to be asked: 'Parandin, this is all beautiful stuff we are talking about. I truly believe it is attainable and had in fact written how it is possible to achieve all that we have talked about in my book *The Six Traits of Self-leadership*. Only please, if you could answer, after you and your family have taken the time to look at and agree on what true success is for you, what is it that stops other people from achieving true success?'

Turning and looking me straight in the eye, she said: 'Michael, if only that was a rhetorical question!' She had a good sense of humour. 'Let's meet in your room in half an hour for coffee. I want to introduce you to someone, and that question will be answered. So, as you go back to your room, please be very mindful of what you see as you walk down the corridor to your suite.'

Heading towards my suite, I did as she asked, and stayed very mindful of what I was seeing. It was as if the embroidered quotes on the wall were jumping out at me. Outside the Ali Suite: 'Friendship . . . is not something you learn in school. But if you haven't learned the meaning of friendship, you really haven't learned anything.' And so it went on as I walked back to my suite. The Su Suite: 'Since we live in this world, we have to do our best for this world.' The Gandhi Suite: 'It is health that is real wealth, and not pieces of gold or silver.' The Frank Suite: 'Laziness may appear attractive, but work gives satisfaction.' The Dawkins Suite: 'By all means let's be open-minded, but not so open-minded that our brains drop out.' The Tutu Suite: 'My humanity is bound up in yours, for we can only be human together.' The Stevens Suite: 'To be what you want to be, you must give up being what you are.' The Hanh Suite: 'When you love someone, the best thing you can offer is your presence. How can you love if you are not there?' The Indira Suite: 'There are two kinds of people: those who do the work and those who take the credit. Try to be in the first group; there is less competition there.' The Frankl Suite: 'Those who have a "why" to live, can bear with almost any "how".' The Hawking Suite: 'However difficult life may seem, there is always something you can do and succeed at.' The O'Connell Suite: 'Nothing is politically right which is morally wrong.'

I was only just back in the room when Parandin knocked on the door and entered, along with another lady, who was carrying our afternoon coffee. 'This is my mother, Madina,' Parandin announced.

Unlike Parandin, Madina did not ask a question (even a rhetorical one!) but instead welcomed me to Hotel Falah. She smiled as she said: 'I will give you an answer to your question, Michael, about how, having identified what it would be to be truly successful, the person doesn't achieve it. It is true that most people really do have the ability and skills to be successful. It's just that they don't have the self-image of themselves as a person who can be truly successful. When they don't believe enough to see themselves being successful, they then have very little chance of achieving true success.

'Your self-image and level of success are always equal. To change your level of success, you must first change your self-image. We have a self-image about everything. It makes us who we are. The sad thing is that most people believe there is nothing they can do: they believe that is the way they are, and they cannot change. In fact, we are changing all the time. We experience change as we age. The direction of that change can either be determined by you or for you. If you do not take control of your life, others surely will.

'When you replace the self-image you have with the self-image you want, you permanently change the success you want for your life. Such a change will take commitment and effort, for the self-image resists change. The only thing is, when you shift the self-image, the change is often permanent.'

'So it's all up to us, I mean, as individuals?' I asked.

'That's right,' she said. 'No one can change your self-image for you. You have to do it yourself.'

'That's huge. Just where do you start?'

Madina continued: 'The first step is to admit that you are not achieving the success you currently wish for in your life. Then you need to believe you are worthy of true success, and gradually your self-image will take you in that direction. The more you think, talk and write about the success you want to happen, the more you increase the probability of that success happening.

'If it feels challenging to even believe you could be successful, start by focusing on the successes you have achieved to date: there will be some. This shows you that you are worthy. Then focus on what it is that you want to happen in the future. Write these goals down in detail; really imagine them as if they were happening, because the self-image cannot tell the difference between what actually happens and what is vividly imagined. Only make sure you also take the actions necessary so that the success you imagine in your mind becomes a reality in your life.

'Also, at the end of each day write down any successes you may have had during that day, however small. This will help build your self-image and increase your chances of attaining success.'

'What about when fears come up?' I asked. 'I'm feeling quite anxious after what Parandin said earlier about the writing and telling of this story, and the pressure I feel to get it right.'

'Yes, Michael, you may be anxious about taking on the writing of this story and getting it out there, but the only thing is, anxiety is fear, and fear is overcome by experience. You have the experience of having already written a book.

'Likewise, pressure is not something you need to avoid. It is something you need to use. Recognise that pressure can be a positive thing, and something you can control. Accept that it is normal to feel pressure in a situation such as writing this book and getting its message out there. The pressure is not in your imagination; it is real. It is your body and mind saying, this is important. Pay attention at such times. When you do feel under pressure, make sure to focus on what you want to see happen, and not on what is causing you stress and making you feel under pressure. When you change your focus, it will change everything for the better. Make sure that your "self-talk" is centred on what you need to do and what you want to happen, as opposed to what you are afraid might happen. Likewise, while others may well choose to beat themselves up when they feel under pressure, you should make sure your self-talk is all about building yourself up.'

Parandin turned to me and said: 'Michael, you drove through Burma – or Myanmar, as it's also known – and you got to stay in Inya Lake?' Yes, I said we had, and we enjoyed a good time there, as it is a truly beautiful, unspoilt place.

'Yes, Michael, it is a beautiful place if you are free to come and go as you please and enjoy all it has to offer: its natural beauty and its facilities, including shops and restaurants. Now, say that you were to be under house arrest for fifteen years, living in a place like that and not able to come and go as you please, not free to enjoy the beauty of Inya Lake and all it has to offer. Well, that was the case for Aung San Suu Kyi*. It was her we looked to for inspiration and hope as we built and set up this hotel. You can see, as soon as you stand in front of this hotel, that the building is so different from all the others surrounding it. I saw the look on your face as you walked from the dining area to your room, and how you enjoyed the sheer beauty and recognised the work that had been done to make this the beautiful hotel it is. I also saw that you wondered how it was that we were able to get the right people to work here, and why it is that we want to share the reasons and the message of why we set up the hotel in the first place. Believe me when I tell you that everything we are trying to do here at Hotel Falah is our way of living lives of true success for us. And this has not come easily. For a start, think of how difficult it was just to get planning permission for the building, let alone all the other challenges and difficulties that we had to face; believe me, there were many in setting up and getting the hotel to the stage it is at now. Yet no matter how difficult it was – and often still is – to live a life of true success, we have looked to Mother Su and taken hope and inspiration from her life and story.

---

* I have no doubt that Parandin and her mum will be, like the rest of us, feeling very disappointed and let down by Aung San Suu Kyi. They will be feeling for the Rohingya people and how they have been made to suffer in Burma. Only as Parandin had said, in our conversation about Steve Jobs, while someone may well be gifted they are human too, like all those here who have suites named after them.

'So, when faced with times of real challenge, make sure you stay motivated and upbeat. Look to your own role models of integrity, inner strength and courage, and make sure that your self-talk, and all that you are thinking, brings you forward to the life of true success that you are meant to live. To help us stay positive and keep going for what we believed was true success for us, we would think of Mother Su and all that she had had to endure so that she was living a life of true success for her.

'We looked to how she was able to withstand fifteen years of house arrest and never lose hope or belief in what it was she stood for. So yes, every time we walk by the suite named after her on your floor, the physical, mental and emotional challenges we went through in completing Hotel Falah pale into insignificance.'

Madina said: 'Yes, there are times in our lives when our circumstances appear to be heading towards doom, but when in reality we are on the road to our dreams; we just don't realise it. I challenge you to look at problems and adversity as learning experiences, to see the potential lesson in every failure, and to appreciate just how fortunate you are. Take successful outcomes as confirmation that you are on the right track, and take unsuccessful ones as opportunities to learn. People, being human, would like whatever they want, to come easy to them; but as you know, this is rarely the case. When things don't go your way, the focus must be on learning from failure, not thinking that you *are* a failure. Also, the truth is that we appreciate things in direct proportion to the price we pay for them.

'Having a real and truly successful life comes down to how much time, effort and energy you are prepared to invest in achieving the successful life you so wish for. It is my duty not to conceal from you the fact that you will meet frustration and disappointment along the way. Like most things that are worth doing, it is not easy, but the rewards are there for you in the end.

'Regardless of what is going on for you, make sure to enjoy the journey and really celebrate taking the small steps that are bringing your life forward. Truly successful people know that it is not just about bringing their life to that successful place they so wish for, it is also as much about how they get there. They know that success is about both the journey and the destination: the challenge is to enjoy both. If you do so, then you will have real and true success in your life.'

'Do you think that people are afraid of success as well as failure?' I asked.

'Yes,' agreed Madina. 'Although many people probably lie awake at night filled with anxiety and self-doubt that they might fail, let's consider the idea that being truly successful may be just as scary. After all, if what you do leads to great success, then you may feel pressure to do it again and again, each time better than the last. Plus, success means that your world might just change, bringing with it new threats, new challenges and new risks. That's world-class frightening. The temptation to sabotage the new thing is huge, precisely because it might work. Instead, when it works for you, push everything else to the side: the noise, the doubts, the anxiety and the confusion. Take what has worked and is working for you, learn from what you did to achieve that success, and then do it again, and keep doing it, in order to maintain the success you have achieved.'

I think back to the beginning of my conversation with Madina, and what she said about the importance of self-worth. I ask her if it becomes easier to believe in yourself as you go along. Does success breed greater self-worth, or does stepping up to the next level challenge our self-worth all over again?

She tells me that you have to keep believing you are worthy of the success you want, especially if you hear that sly voice whispering in your ear telling you: *You don't have a clue what you're doing.*

You just got lucky this time. You will be found out: it's all going to go wrong.

'Just before the achievement of true and real success (regardless of the area it is in life), one will often experience some form of difficulty, which, if not dealt with in a proper manner, might lead to you sabotaging the opportunity. If you find yourself in this situation, the key is to maintain your focus and keep on believing in your definition of success, and in your own worthiness of having this success in your life. If you start to doubt yourself, remember to look at what you have achieved thus far, and to see how much further along the path you are than you were before, and how important it is to keep going.'

I thanked her for everything, then said: 'What is happening here is just amazing. In fact, I can't make any sense of it all at this time, but I know I am listening to precious beliefs and treading on sacred ground while I am here.'

Madina said she was delighted to have met me, and so glad that I was writing about what it is to live a life of true and real success. 'While it may seem overwhelming now, Michael, it will all make sense when you come to write about your experiences and our conversations here at Hotel Falah.'

With that, the two of them excused themselves, as they had to go back to work. As they left, I waited for the next question, and when none was forthcoming, I just had to ask: 'No question, not even a rhetorical one?'

They both smiled at that, and as they turned to me, Madina said: 'Think over what it is we have just talked about, for that is enough for now.' Parandin just said she would be working in the restaurant, and please would I come for dinner; she would be able to meet me for a coffee during her break. I thanked them both as they left, and said I would see her then.

24 November, on the border between Thailand and Malaysia

It is almost time to say goodbye to 'the Village'. This truck, which has been our home for the last nineteen weeks, is to be parked up in Kuala Lumpur, as the group is taking public transport to Singapore for the weekend, before flying on to Indonesia, where they will stay for a week. They will then fly to Darwin and drive across Australia to Sydney, arriving on the 19th of December, if all goes to plan.

We have all grown fond of 'the Village'. It has looked after us; we have told jokes, enjoyed stunning views and made life-long memories as it wended its way along the highways and byways of Europe, Asia and South-east Asia.

There is a lump in my throat and I'm feeling sad, although not just about leaving 'the Village'. Once we get to Singapore, I will be saying a final goodbye to the group, to whom I have become very close. My plan is to stay in Singapore for as long as it takes to write my book. Although I am excited about staying in one place and really getting down to my writing, I am disappointed that I won't continue on with the rest of the group to the journey's end in Sydney.

Billy and I stand there looking at 'the Village' affectionately. Then he turns to me and says: 'Coming on this trip, and in particular seeing Myanmar, was the fulfilment of a dream: it has changed my life. I had to muster up the courage to come on this trip, as I was tempted just to look for a job straight away after being made redundant. I felt like such a failure. So much of my self-image was wrapped up in my work, to the extent that I didn't even realise it. But when I thought about it, I knew that if I didn't come on this trip now, I never would. I also knew that I would never be able to look myself in the mirror again if I didn't come.'

Success is not an accident, I think to myself. Billy tells me that he had thought, talked about and imagined doing this adventure for the last five years. He said that it had taken him that long to build up his self-belief to the point where he could allow himself to actually do it.

'Just like this one we are on, success is a journey,' I say to him. 'It's the same with my book. I'm not sure I really believe in myself enough – which is why it has taken so long for me to decide how and what to write, so that it felt true to me.'

Billy goes on to tell me how he got into the habit of picturing positive images about this trip, which was critical for him. For positive pictures demand positive results from the subconscious, and as you are picturing something positive it is impossible, at the same time, to picture something negative; but you have to be vigilant and focused about it.

'Yes,' he says. 'I looked at myself in the mirror and decided that I was going to take a stand for my life. I realised that if I really wanted to come on this journey, it was up to me. I had to take responsibility for my own life. Once I did that, I was finally able to make the call to book and pay for the trip. It was a wonderful moment, knowing that I was going on a journey from London to Sydney.'

Billy adds, 'I've felt unsuccessful so many other times in my life, but not this time, because what I'm doing is so meaningful to me, and my courage has just grown and grown. It took a lot for me to come on this trip, but now we are almost at the end of the journey, what feels even bigger is not just coming on the trip, but the fact that I stayed on it!

'Looking back now, I realise that coming on the trip was the easy part! The physical challenge of constantly travelling and always being on the move has really got me down at times. I've also missed home comforts like easy access to washing facilities, toilets and "proper food". I like simple food, and having to eat what we did made me quite unwell at times. Even thinking about it still makes me feel sick: the sheep lungs that I ate in Iran, the chicken's feet in some kind of sauce in Chin, and the beef cooked over a fire beside an open drain in Myanmar! Yet I kept going.

'I'm someone who likes to keep myself to myself, and living in such close contact with other people has proved to be a massive challenge.'

I nod in agreement with this, as four of our group have already left – for many of the reasons Billy has just outlined – and two more won't make it to Sydney due to personal issues back home. But Billy has made it this far, and says: 'I kept going in spite of everything, and I will keep going, and stay to the end.' He says this with such conviction that we both know in that moment that he will make it all the way to Sydney (and he does).

As we stand there taking one last photo of 'the Village', he goes on to say: 'You are probably wondering what is next for me when I get back home.' I nod, for Billy is a good guy, and I genuinely wish him the best in life. 'I'm not going back to banking: that decision has been made. I have had enough of the corporate life and would now like to devote the rest of my career to use all that I have learnt from my banking life in the pursuit of helping others. I'm going to do my best to go and work with a charity.' Again there is such certainty in his voice as he says this that we both know this is going to become a reality for him when he does get back home. Billy exercised his 'courage-muscle' big-time by coming on, and then staying on, this trip, and I feel inspired that he is going to keep taking steps to move forward with his life in a positive way.

In fact, what Billy said gives me renewed energy and enthusiasm for writing my book. For it is my *book and no one else's. I feel a true sense of ownership and a responsibility for making it my own. And when I have written this book, I will go out and share it with the world.*

Conversation Eight
How do you make success a way of life?

I thought back to Madina's words: 'While it may seem overwhelming now, Michael, it will all make sense when you come to write about your experiences and our conversations here at Hotel Falah.' In other words, it was as if the story was writing itself and I was only the channel between what Hotel Falah represented and the written words on the pages of my book. For now, I decided to relax and take advantage of that luxurious bathtub before going to dinner.

*

After dinner, Parandin met me for a coffee in the lobby during her break. She too acknowledged that achieving success is challenging, particularly when it seems so far away. She said that, paradoxically, the greater challenge is that, having achieved success, you will not have the commitment and dedication to stay focused on what needs to be done to maintain it.

'Every individual is vulnerable, no matter how successful they are,' she said. 'No matter how far they have brought their life forward, or how much success they have achieved, they are vulnerable to decline and failure. There is no law of nature that the most successful will inevitably remain successful. Anyone can fail – and most eventually do, if they haven't learned how to maintain success, having achieved it.'

Now I was really feeling the pressure! Nonetheless, I felt so lucky. I told her that after all our conversations, I was starting to feel like the book I had set out to write upon leaving London would write itself (even though I had yet to complete a first draft!).

Parandin said that this was great news. She had to go back to work but said that she and her mother would like to have a farewell breakfast with me in the morning: all that they had to share with me was nearly done. She had been in touch with our mutual friend, Emma, asking her to let the rest of the group know that my time at Hotel Falah was coming to an end. It would therefore be possible for me to join up with the group at the airport the next morning to travel to Indonesia for the week, before flying on to Darwin and then driving across Australia, to finish in Sydney on the 19th of December.

Although I was sorry that I would soon be leaving Hotel Falah, it also felt natural to be rejoining the group and seeing out the rest of this mad adventure we were all on. In fact, I was amazed at how well timed everything had been, with this enlightening and unexpected detour simply fitting into the overall journey, almost as if somebody had planned it that way!

I said that I would very much welcome the chance to have breakfast with Parandin and her mother, and that there was one final question that needed to be asked before finishing up there. She excused herself, saying she really was needed back in the restaurant, but that the question would be answered in the morning – and with that, once again, she was gone.

But I never had the time to tell her what the question was, so how could she know?

29 November, Hotel Falah, Singapore

I am sitting in the hotel library, a place of tranquillity, surrounded by a huge number of books from all over the world. It is only just starting to sink in that I have experienced some amazing new worlds over the past few months. A kaleidoscope of cultures, religions, people, societies, beliefs and civilisations on this journey along the Silk Road. And while this magical journey so far has been life-enhancing, it hasn't fully prepared me for what it is I'm experiencing here at Hotel Falah. Yet I have a sense that because of this journey and my time here in Singapore, I am not only ready to write this story but, more importantly, to actually go and live it.

I feel truly grateful for being here, and for all that I have heard so far from Parandin about what she and her people believe it is to live a life of true success. This hotel has played host to some world-renowned people: statesmen and women, politicians, church and holy figures, business people, warriors and rebels, royalty, researchers, scientists, sailors, fishermen, artists, musicians, athletes and writers. Yet here I am, staying as a guest of Parandin, her mother and their people.

Call it what you like – divine providence, synchronicity – it doesn't matter, for whichever way you look at it, the fact is that I am here and a challenge has been laid down: write this story, and go and tell the world about it. I have agonised over not giving my agent what he wanted me to write about success, and have thought about the consequences of losing a publishing deal. Only now, I am so happy that I push the noise and confusion in my head to one side. I am delighted that I have listened to myself on a gut level and am responding to the challenge of believing in myself and doing what feels right for me and my book. When I first made that decision, some doubts kicked in, and I wondered if I would really be able to write a book on the meaning of true success.

In truth, though, all I had to do was 'get out of my own way' by putting aside my doubts: the book is beginning to write itself. It is now feeling like the easiest book in the world to write because of all the great and wonderful knowledge Parandin has shared with me.

Sitting here in the library, I do feel as though I am at a crossroads in my life, for now I want to be more than I have been. I fully understand and accept that I, and I alone, must decide what it is for me to live a life of true success: this has become very clear to me during my time at Hotel Falah.

I am realising that I want to write and teach what Parandin has shared with me during my time here. If I want to do this, then I have to have the courage, determination and self-belief to go and make this a reality in my own life. I need to believe in myself as a writer and teacher.

Looking around at the bookshelves, I think about the question I still have for Parandin and her mother. I start smiling to myself about the fact that they both know what that question is, even though I have yet to ask it – and in the next moment, I realise that I already know the answer.

Parting Words
Be the best that you can be

I awoke the next morning having had a restless night. The only thing was, I did not feel tired. Yes, the strange sense of anxiety and fear that I had felt the night before was still there, but at the same time I was looking forward to hearing what Parandin and her mother were going to say in answer to the questions that kept going around in my head:

- Why did they both want me to write the book?
- Would I be able to write this story and do it justice?
- Having written it, would I be able to get it out into the world so it could reach those who needed to hear this story?

In expectation of another great conversation with them both, I jumped out of bed. I was no sooner out of the shower than Parandin and her mother were knocking on the door with breakfast for all of us.

As if reading my mind, Madina said: 'Yes, of course you will do justice to all that has happened during your stay here at Hotel Falah. The only thing we want for you, Michael, is to be the best that you can possibly be. It doesn't matter what level of talent has

75

been given to us, what size we are, or how fast or slow we run. It is always about what we *do* with the talent that we have that counts, with no excuses and no exceptions: that you do the best you can with the writing of this story and letting people hear it, nothing more and nothing less.'

'It does feel like a great challenge to write this story and get it out there,' I said.

'Yes, it probably does,' Madina agreed. 'But this is what makes true success special. We tend to value things in direct proportion to the price we pay for them. There is no doubt that you will have a lot of challenges along your journey of writing this story. Indeed, I hope you do, for dealing with and overcoming resistance makes you stronger. We believe that by challenging you to write this story, we are honouring that which you are capable of becoming. It will lead to you being great rather than just good, playing a bigger game, a more expansive game, a more ambitious game. We have to leave this world in a better place for us having been there, and this is one way for you to do that, Michael.

'What you leave behind is not what is engraved in stone monuments, to paraphrase the Greek statesman Pericles, but what is woven into the lives of others. Let your legacy be that which you teach from having written this story. Yes, you may be fearful about doing justice to and honouring all that has been shared with you during your time here, but as you write, make sure to focus on what it is you desire, and not what you lack, and you will succeed in getting this story out there.

'Even though life won't always work out the way you want it to, you must remain optimistic if you want to be successful. Also, be grateful and do your best to recognise all that is good in your life, for this is the greatest gift you can give to yourself.

'If at times you find yourself feeling down because the true success you desire isn't happening, then start to look for benefits (of any type – big or small) in the situation or circumstances that you find yourself in, regardless of how bad they are. If you persist in doing this, even after repeated failure, then you will not only start to feel optimistic, but you will achieve success, and also be able to maintain it.

'So, go on, Michael, and have the courage to write this story and get it out there. There are times in our lives when we have to bite the bullet and just go for it – be courageous. Far too many people wait until they pluck up the courage before taking action. If you find yourself in this situation, you need to tune in to your intuition, so that you can feel your way forward even if you don't have all the information or know all the steps to take in advance.

'Life is all about not knowing, Michael, but then having the courage to go for it anyway. All of life is like this. And in the long run it doesn't get any easier just because you've written your book or you love your job (regardless of what it is you are doing) or you win the Lottery – whatever your equivalent of winning the Lottery is.

'As to why we allowed you into our world and want you to tell this story? Well, that's simple, Michael. There is an old nomadic saying that the wise man isn't he who has lived the most, but he who has travelled the most. So having travelled the Silk Road yourself, you have a real understanding of what it is to travel, as our family have travelled over all these generations. Equally, you never know what might happen if you keep an open mind and an open heart as you tell this story.' She smiled as she said this.

'Once you write this book, who knows how many people it may inspire to discover for themselves what true success would mean, and then decide to go live it? Whatever your present situation, I assure you that you can live a life of true success. You can let the past go and replace it with a sense of the true success that you would now like in all areas of your life.

'Michael, if you want to predict where someone is going, don't look at where they've been, look at what they are doing in their life now. What you do each day is building the future, even though you may not see the results right away.'

'So I need to be present with each day?' I asked.

'That's right. Be aware of whatever is happening in your life in the present moment; today this may well be known as being mindful. This can, and will, help you respond to the challenges and demands being placed on you in a calmer manner that will benefit your heart, head and body. It will help you cultivate clarity, insight and understanding, and will also help you improve the quality of your life and relationships.'

Her words reinforced something that I have been aware of since my training to be a monk more than twenty-five years ago: the art of being present in the moment. So, every day since leaving the monastery, I do my best to spend some time meditating. Having a very active mind, as I do, journalling has also been a great way for me to clear my mind and become present in the moment; so I do this every morning upon waking and in the evening before going to bed. When that isn't possible, such as when I'm travelling and have very little space, time or opportunity, I have found that going for a walk is another great way of becoming present in the moment and really appreciating this journey of life that I am on.

Madina continued: 'Most people spend very little time living in the present. A lot of the time they are focused on past experiences and living with regrets – which can lead to depression. Or they try to anticipate the future, wondering what it might hold; this often leads them to feel stressed and anxious rather than them trying to create their successful future. By becoming more present, and living in the now, you begin to see situations and all that is going on in your life more clearly; as you become more aware of your body, you will also strengthen your immune system, improving your performance in all areas of your life, and enhancing your relationships.

'So take some time to be silent and quieten the mind. Slow your breathing down and be grounded in the present moment. When you do this, you have a greater chance of becoming mindful of who, what and where you are, and you will experience increased joy, success and contentment in your life. There is an often-held view that our past largely determines the person we have become; yet who we were in the past and who we are in the present does not necessarily determine the person we will become in the future. Remember, your past does not equal your future: you and everyone else can only accomplish true success in the present – or at least lay the foundations for a successful future.'

I felt this really soft, peaceful place in my mind as I listened to her answer the questions that had been so much in my thoughts the night before. I stared directly into her eyes and saw hope – hope for the future. She really had managed to deliver me to a state where I saw everything in a light that was crystal clear: it was possible to tell this story, and let the world know about it. Madina must have sensed this, for she took her leave, wishing me the very best for the future. But before she went, she explained that they had done all they could for me, and that while she was happy for me to mention her and Parandin by name, all else with regard to the family and the actual hotel was to be kept strictly between us. She did not want people to be caught up in how the hotel sees success for itself (as people might believe that this would constitute success for them too); instead, people should take inspiration from it and then pursue their own unique and true success.

All that was left now was for Parandin and me to say our goodbyes. I was sad to be saying goodbye to her as our time together drew to a close. I knew that I would never forget the spirit of what had been shared with me. I would remember her and her mother's request that I go and get on with my life, and they go and get on with theirs.

'So, what about you and the future of the hotel?' I asked. She smiled warmly. 'We will see how things work out. There is the immediate challenge of making sure that Hotel Falah lives up to its name, for as I have told you, *falah* is the Arabic word for success.

'However, it is not the business that is important, but the family, true relationships and true friendships, and our children (for those of us who are fortunate to have them) that are most important. This is what true success is for me.'

All that was left was for me to wish her the very best for the future and say thank you. She replied: 'Thank you, Michael, for the guest is even greater than your father.' I recognised this as an Uzbekistan proverb from the Silk Road, meaning that your host has played the role of servant to you, yet acknowledges that you have treated them as an equal. From the very first moment we met, it was as equals, and I had always treated her as an equal, even after finding out she was the owner's daughter! It was so moving to have her put me in the same company as her father, knowing that he had passed away. She smiled, we gave each other a hug, and then she was gone.

In many ways, Parandin had treated me much like her own father; she was without doubt the warmest and most interesting person I had ever met. She and her mother had set before me a massive challenge; only, in that moment, I felt inexplicable serenity. In this new state of mind, I knew that it was possible to go and tell this story. With that, I picked up my rucksack, gave one last look around the hotel, knowing that I would never see it again, and checked out.

Sitting in the taxi on the way to the airport to meet up with what was left of the gang before continuing on our journey to Sydney, I thought back to what Parandin and her mother had shared with me throughout all these conversations. I took out a notebook to see if I could capture the essence of all that we had discussed. I wrote:

- Take the time to look internally. Let this be the fountain from which all knowledge and understanding flows as to the meaning of the true success you want for your life.

- Accept that it is your life, so take responsibility for turning the true success you desire into reality; living a truly successful life also means being present in each moment as you do this.
- Being truly successful is also about legacy, whether you inspire others by your own example or through something meaningful you create in the world.

Or as Paradin once said to me: 'Know the way and go the way.'

Getting out of the taxi and stepping back into the noise and chaos of the airport terminal seemed a world away from the tranquillity of the hotel and the depth of our conversations, but for the first time on this trip it really felt like I and my book were on our way.

EPILOGUE

Standing in Dublin Airport on a cold January day waiting to collect my rucksack, I cannot quite believe that it really is all over.

Leaving Singapore, the remaining members of the group travelled through Indonesia and then on to Darwin before driving across Australia to finish the journey in Sydney. There we went our separate ways, with some continuing their travels in Australia and others flying back to their home countries. I stayed in Sydney for the next three weeks, recalling and writing down what had happened during my time with Parandin.

I have had lots of time to reflect on my experiences at Hotel Falah, as well as all that happened on my overland adventure from London to Sydney.

My most challenging journey now really was over – or was it? In a short time, I would once again be back to all my usual comforts of home – some of which I missed, like my own bed and bedroom, as well as having my own space to pretty much come and go as I pleased. The thought of seeing family and friends was more powerful than I had imagined it would be; I had so many stories to tell them. In particular, I had to write this book.

As Madina told me: 'The wise person isn't the one who has lived the most, but the one who has travelled the most.' I believe she really meant that it was the journey inwards, and not necessarily outwards, that made you wise, and yet for me this journey had been about both. I felt as though I had been on a quest.

I had physically travelled from one side of the world to the other, hoping to discover what to write in my book about true success. All my conversations with Parandin had allowed me to look inwards to find out what true success meant for me.

In truth, though, I had returned to Ireland with a heavy heart. It was as if Parandin knew this would be the case: 'If you listen to your head and don't write this book – wanting to just keep it there for yourself – then you would be choosing the easier path. You know that this story has to be shared; the book has to be written.' Or at least that is how I interpreted her words. There was a conflict between my head and my heart which I had to deal with myself, for in reality no one, and nothing, else was going to make this situation any easier for me. Perhaps because there was no way to make it easier, I had to go through with the whole painful process of taking responsibility for seeing this book become a reality; I had to take responsibility for doing justice to both Parandin and her story, and to myself, by writing the book that was truly in me. As I accepted this responsibility, I experienced an amazing moment of liberation.

I did listen to my heart, for while there was at times a pull to keep this story and my conversations with Parandin and her mother to myself, the truth was that this was never my story to keep, for it was told to me as one to be shared. Only as I wrote the story, I had to both listen to and follow the advice of my mind as to how best to write the story and get it out into the world.

One afternoon, as I put a full stop at the end of a sentence, I lifted my hands from the keyboard and saw that they were shaking. This was the first time I had fully recalled my time with Parandin, seeing the hotel, my suite, and her, in my mind's eye. As I was writing, my time in Hotel Falah was all crystal clear, and her words rang in my ears all over again, along with her challenge to go and tell this story. I realised that any fear I had had with regard to doing justice to her and her family's traditions, which had been handed from generation to generation, had lessened.

Writing this book has allowed me to get the story inside me out into the light; in a strange way, it has also allowed for a continuation of what was started in my first book. It has allowed the telling of the story of Parandin, her people and Hotel Falah, hopefully written in such a way as to do justice to them. The story lets me know I was there, just as many braver men and women beforehand were also there, somewhere, unknowingly, on the Silk Road in search of what true success was for them.

What has this journey, and my time with Parandin, taught me about what true success means to me? It many ways, it has been a real mixture of reaffirming some things I already knew, such as being more grateful for the life already being lived; but it has also been about coming to both a greater understanding of true success and a realisation of what it means for me to live a life of true success.

My work in future will take me in a different direction, as a result of having met Parandin and heard her people's story. The journey that I had set out on from London had been about writing a book, only now it has proved to be so much more than that. Yes, the book is written, and having finished it, my life will now be about sharing its messages: how Parandin and her people see true success, and what it is that you must do to see this true success become a reality within your own life. I came to write a book and I did; only now I have found a new purpose for my life. I also understand how to build my self-esteem to allow this purpose to become the driving force of my life, so that it will be one of true success. I will now be living a very simple life, one that focuses on living my purpose: I am that writer, I am that teacher, and that is my purpose in life now.

I accept that many will be sceptical about what is written here, such as those who see success as something external. That's OK, though, because I know that true success comes from within, and I will continue to build up my own self-image to support myself and those who want to live a life of true success, a different type of success. I intend to go now to live every day to the best of my ability, regardless of the circumstances I may find myself in, not only in getting this book out into the world, but in other areas of my life too.

There is a need to be truly grateful for my good health and the hobbies I am able to enjoy; for so many others, life is a struggle just to make ends meet. I will stop taking these things for granted, for they can be taken away in the blink of an eye. The truth is that this was something that I did know, but I only came to realise it fully after I had sat down to write this book and reflect on my journey.

I will be thankful for the family that has made me the person I am, and for the small number of close friends I have. I need to accept that living a life pursuing the true success I want may well mean that I have to lose some friends and colleagues along the way – and that this is also OK, as other, newer ones will come into my life. These new friends and colleagues will be better placed, and better suited, to what I am now doing with my life, and will understand how best they can support me. Equally, as I pursue true success I will come into the lives of others who will need my understanding and support, whether I give it personally or professionally – whatever is best suited to meet their needs. Finally, I will appreciate my good fortune to be living in a good street with really great neighbours.

I now know and accept that in the end, all that will count is how I spent my time on this earth, and how much of my time and energy I used in the pursuit of living a life of true success.

Thinking about and answering Parandin's questions also made me ask myself: am I in fact here to be happy? Or might it be that I am here to become a better person, to achieve my true potential and make a better world, and only in so doing will I find true success?

As I travelled the journey from one side of the world to the other, had the discussions with Parandin, answered her questions, and wrote this book, I have come to firmly believe that yes, I am here to be happy, only not at any cost; this happiness should not come at the price of transgressing the natural laws of fairness with regard to all those with whom I come into contact. If I live my life in this way, then, yes, I can be happy and yet at the same time become a better person, achieve my true potential and make a better world; in doing so, true success will become a reality for me. As I now go forward with my life, I will do my best to have faith in Jesus Christ, for the more I put into knowing him, the closer I really do feel to God, and the better I understand what it is to live a good life, a truly successful life.

All my conversations with Parandin have helped me realise the importance of self-image, and to see that if I do not believe in myself, I will have very little chance of being truly successful. I now know that if I do not have an image of myself as someone who can live a life of true success, then I need to change my self-image. Although this is difficult, it can be done. So, every day I now look in the mirror and see myself as someone who is worthy of true success. I also think, write and talk about the true success I want for my life – for what we focus on becomes our reality.

Writing this book and getting this story out into the world has played a huge part in boosting my self-image, and I know that this will also spread to other areas of my life.

At the same time, I am keeping in mind that there will be moments when it will seem as though I am living a life of true success, and other moments when it will seem that the opposite is the case. At times like this, I need to remember moments of success which can be built on, one on top of another, giving me a real sense of fulfilment, so that I know what it is to live a life of true success.

I believe that the pursuit of those things that many people may think will make them successful in our consumer society – notably fame, power and wealth – are less likely to make people truly successful than to give them a sense of elation, which rarely endures. Whereas in reality, it is the people who are living a life of true success who have understood all the ingredients for successful living: a real sense about the life they want to live; the courage to go and do their best to live this life; faith in both themselves and in a higher power; a sense of humour; gratitude for all that is good within their lives; and an understanding of and compassionate recognition for all those with whom they come into contact. If success is to be real and true, and not just a one-off event, these things should all be lived out, day in, day out.

Now discover what
TRUE SUCCESS MEANS FOR YOU

I do hope that reading this book has inspired you to discover what true success is for you. I now invite you to ask yourself the questions that Parandin asked me, so you can begin your own journey to discover what true success means to you.

So, please allow yourself first of all to switch off and take the time out to ask what you need from life, in order for it to be one of true success. How best can you switch off? For me, it is to read, travel, meditate, journal and walk in nature (even within the city). Try different things, and discover what works best for you.

Then I invite you to consider Parandin's questions. You can start with the first one – what does true success mean to you – and then work your way through them in order. Or you can choose any particular one that you feel most drawn to exploring. Either way, the most important thing is to give yourself the time and space to consider the questions, and to see what answers come up for you.

Whichever way you do it, I suggest that you work through her questions one at a time, slowly, without over-thinking them. Above all, do not rush or force the answers. Let them come naturally to you – and they will, if you allow yourself the time and space! For example, when I have selected one of her questions, I allow myself time to switch off and mull it over, using any or all of the above techniques that work best for me, namely reading, travelling, meditating, journalling and walking in nature.

Allow your inner thoughts and feelings to come forward like a compass showing you the way, because as we know, true success is inner-led. If you allow your true answer to reveal itself, then you will substantially increase the chances of you having true success in your life, both now and in the future.

Having worked your way through Parandin's questions, and having ascertained what true success means to you, then ask yourself: do you feel worthy of this success?

Understanding the importance of self-worth and feeling good about yourself is all tied in to your core beliefs. Also, it is important to appreciate that we all have a comfort-zone, whether that relates to money, health, leaving a legacy, or something else. So when you change your self-image, your comfort-zone shifts. As Parandin and I discussed in our third conversation, about whether we feel worthy of true success, there is a need here also to work continually at strengthening your 'muscles of proactivity'. Take the necessary actions to keep moving forward with your life, in the belief that you are worthy of achieving true success in all areas of your life.

If you struggle when it comes to believing in your own worth, you must be prepared to look yourself in the mirror and work on building up your self-image, as it makes you who you are. The level of success you have in your life is always equal to your self-image. There is no avoiding this inner work: without it, you will struggle to achieve the success you desire, or you will sabotage what you do achieve.

If you are finding it hard to believe in yourself, then start by making a note of past successes. Then think about the success you would like to have in all the different areas of your life. Even thinking about success happening, improves the probability that it will happen.

Next, list your goals: writing down what you want to happen will aid the building of your self-image as a successful person, and give you a greater chance of achieving it.

Picture your success, and see it happening in your mind's eye. Having positive pictures will demand positive results from the subconscious.

At the end of each day, write down what has gone well, rather than focusing on what did not.

Decide to think, talk and write about the success you want, and then go and take the action needed in your life every day in order to see your true success become a reality.

As you progress towards your goals, you may come up against some negative beliefs about yourself that just will not shift. If you do, work to clear these. If they are deep-rooted, you may need some outside help to do this; but whatever you do, be gentle with yourself and keep moving towards your goals just the same. Simply deciding to improve your self-belief sends a message to your sub-conscious that you are a worthy person.

Remember too that following your true success may mean hav-ing to reject what it is your culture, conditioning and peer-group define as success for you. This too will require a strong sense of self-worth, and you will also need to build up a supportive network of people around you.

As you now go forward with your life, develop a positive out-look, knowing that this will help you to understand and accept that you are much stronger and more resilient than you believe; this will help you to make the true success you want for your life become a reality. Regardless of the circumstances you may find yourself in, be they good or challenging, remember always to have a sense of gratitude.

Make sure to give yourself time and space to stay true to finding out what you love to do and how you want to make this a part of your life, so that you can go on to make yours a life of true success. You will often find yourself in inhospitable terrain. Look within yourself for guidance rather than seeking outside approval, or looking at what others are doing or listening to, or what the world at large says you need to be doing.

For what you do, and how you live your life, can be your legacy – a legacy to yourself in how you truly valued yourself, as well as the contribution you made in this world. Accept that living a successful life is a legacy in itself, as you are an example to others. Understand that as you live your life in this way, you will in all probability create an actual legacy out in the world.

If you find yourself getting anxious about the future, or thinking of the past, there is a need to be mindful of living in the present moment. This is achieved in different ways for different people. For me, it is about breathing deeply and becoming aware of my breathing, so as to regulate it, taking in deep breaths and making long exhalations. This often works for people like me, who are active-minded.

Those who find it hard to focus on breathing often use imagery, like a bird flying freely in the sky or a field full of blooming poppies, or picture themselves standing on a beach facing the sun on a beautiful warm day.

Others use words or phrases like a mantra to get them into the moment and keep them focusing on the present: repeating over and over something like 'I love knowing my life is working out brilliantly'. The trick is to come up with something that works specifically for you. For you too could find something that you can use that will hold your focus, so you become grounded in the present. Others find it easier to sing a short song lyric to help them come into the present. They choose words from a song that resonates with them, and they sing these in their mind over and over again.

Success comes before work only in the dictionary. Those who have achieved, or are in the process of achieving, true success understand it is a process, and not just like turning on a light-switch. When you set out in pursuit of the success you want for your life, it really is true that it will take much longer than you could have ever anticipated; for that reason, you can be assured that it was a worthy form of success that you pursued. Also, the harder you have to work for something, the greater value you will place on it, having achieved it.

Equally, when it comes to true success, it is difficult to feel that you are ever really finished or completely successful in all aspects of your life at all times. Your life is a work in progress. The important thing to remember is that you, and you alone, can decide what true success means to you and your life. You are free to choose.

Choosing to write this book in the way that I wanted to, that felt right for me, has shown me that when it comes to true success in your own life, you can make any choice you want. There is nothing to hold you back any more. When you let go of how the world defines success and follow the success that is right and true for you, then anything can happen. Anything! Try it, and you will see – for this is your moment.

'*Know the way and go the way.*'

Parandin

The Six Traits of Self-Leadership
A summary

I hope that reading this book will inspire you to discover the meaning of true success for you. If you would then like some guidance on how to achieve it, you may want to read my first book, *The Six Traits of Self-leadership: How to Create a Life of Success and Happiness.*

People who are following a path of true success are self-leaders. The book outlines the six key traits they share, which help them to bring that success into all areas of their lives.

Here is a short summary of them:

Trait 1: Being Determined is all about being prepared to face your fears (we all have them, and there are some of which we may be unaware), take risks and be optimistic as you pursue the success you want in your life. Problems and challenges will come up, but you can overcome these. Optimism is the one quality most frequently linked to having success.

Trait 2: Getting Creative explains the need for rest and renewal, both in mind and body, if you want to come up with new ideas, projects and adventures, and then follow them through to successful completion. It also discusses how creativity can show you the way to success.

Trait 3: Playing to Your Strengths is all about focusing on those talents and skills where you already have a certain level of natural ability, and making them even stronger. If you build on your strengths rather than trying to fix your weaknesses, then you are on the road to true success.

Trait 4: Having a Vision for Your Life and Work discusses the importance of defining the success that you want. This gives you something positive to aim for, brings focus to your efforts, gives you a greater sense of self-worth, guides your decision-making, and gives meaning and purpose to your life. The key is to make sure that your vision touches your heart and soul, and really motivates you.

Trait 5: Knowing Your Mission is all about how you need to have a personal mission statement to support the vision of success you want to achieve and how to take ownership of it. It is a practical guide, with priorities and goals that will keep you on track, and also help you to align your behaviour with your beliefs in pursuit of your vision. Rather than reacting to what happens, you are able to respond to situations and challenges on the road to your success.

Trait 6: Staying Focused is really about making sure you are not pulled in every direction, only in the direction that matters most to you. Achieving success is not just a matter of getting things done, but getting the *right* things done. Knowing what you want to achieve, and staying focused, will push you to take action to accomplish what is important to you, rather than what is important to others.

If you would like to read more about these traits, then please do check out my book *The Six Traits of Self-leadership: How to Create a Life of Success and Happiness*.